George Trumbull Ladd

What is the Bible? An Inquiry into the Origin and Nature of the

Old and New Testaments in the Light of modern Biblical Study

George Trumbull Ladd

What is the Bible? An Inquiry into the Origin and Nature of the Old and New Testaments in the Light of modern Biblical Study

ISBN/EAN: 9783743332744

Manufactured in Europe, USA, Canada, Australia, Japa

Cover: Foto ©Lupo / pixelio.de

Manufactured and distributed by brebook publishing software
(www.brebook.com)

George Trumbull Ladd

What is the Bible? An Inquiry into the Origin and Nature of the Old and New Testaments in the Light of modern Biblical Study

CONTENTS.

The Vision of Jesus Christ.(chap. 1.)

The Epistles of Christ, the universal Bishop, to the seven Churches in Asia; extending through all Time to the Coming of our Lord. (chaps. II and III.)

Christ revealed as a King seated on a Throne in Heaven (chap. IV.)

Christ revealed as a Priest, the Lamb slain from the Foundations of the World. (chap. V.)

The first Series of Judgments inflicted on the Western Branch of the Roman Empire. (chap. VI.)

The sealing of the British Nation from the Effects of the Seventh Seal. (chap. VII.)

The Judgments and final Overthrow of the Church in the Eastern Branch of the Roman Empire. (chaps VIII and IX.)

Christ exhibited as the Inflictor of Judgments. (chap. X.)

Epitome of the Church History. (chap. XI)

History of the Church during the Pagan Period, being that of the fourth Beast of Daniel, or the Roman Empire when under Paganism. (chap. XII.)

History of the Church during the Papal Period, when the Roman Empire is divided into the Ten Kingdoms of Great Britain, France, Austria, Spain, Portugal, Naples, Sardinia, and the three Ecclesiastical States of Rome, Ravenna, and Lombardy. (chap. XIII.)

The Acts of the True Church during the first Period of the Infidel Ascendancy in the Roman Empire. (chap. XIV.)

Supplementary History, containing the Seven last Vials of Wrath the sevenfold Act of Vengeance, commencing A. D. 1792. (chaps. XV. and XVI.)

History of the Roman Empire under its last Form of Infidelity,
    and during the Supremacy of the Infidel Antichrist. (chap.
    XVII.)

Judgment on Babylon the Great, the Mother of Harlots and
    Abominations of the Earth. (chap. XVIII.)

Final Confederation of the Ten Papal Kings under their Leader,
    the Infidel Antichrist, who is the eighth Head of the Beast
    yet of the seven.   The coming of our Lord with all his Saints;
    the fate of the Infidel Antichrist and the False Prophet of
Rome, and the utter Destruction of the Ten Papal Kings, with
    heir confederate Armies. (chap. XIX.)

PREFACE TO THIS EDITION.

THIS condensed, but comprehensive, work was first published in London, in 1829.

In a comparative small compass it contains the substance of the large and expensive works of Fleming, Jones, Frere, Dr. Cumming, Elliott, and other writers on Prophecy.

The work had a great circulation in England and Scotland, but is supposed to be now out of print, which has induced the Editor and Publisher of this Edition to lay it again before the public in a cheap and popular form.

What will render this work of great interest to the Religious Public of the present day is the fact, that much which necessarily was conjecture with the Author in 1829, is now a matter of History in 1860—and the inference is therefore fair, that what is still unfulfilled may be as literally fulfilled.

There is no doubt that the great Religious Revival which is now going on in many parts of Europe, America, and Asia, is a work of the Holy Spirit—to prepare the Church for the speedy advent of our Lord—and that the cry may possibly now have gone forth *"Behold the Bridegroom cometh."* In which case, does it not become the duty of the *"Wise Virgins"* to be trimming their Lamps and be prepared to enter in before the *"Door is shut."*

Should this little work, in any way, aid in this great and important preparation, the end desired by the re-publication of this Book will have, in so far, been obtained by,

THE EDITOR.

Galt, 8th February, 1860.

PREFACE.

It is admitted by all commentators, that the prophecies contained in the Revelations to St. John at Patmos are of a far more enlarged and comprehensive character, and include ampler revelations of the will and purpose of God, than is to be found in any other prophecy contained in the inspired volume. The object for which this prophecy is given to the Christian Church through the beloved disciple is evidently of a consolatory character, and calculated to cheer the prospects and animate the courage of the Church, during those various vicissitudes and persecutions which should attend her footsteps under the brutal oppression of the fourth beast of Daniel, or the Roman Empire, in its Pagan, Papal, and Infidel form of government; and extending through all the history of the Church, until Christ himself should come and deliver his saints from the dominion of the fourth beast, when the time should arrive when the kingdom over the whole earth should be given unto the Son of Man, and to the Saints of the Most High God, who are to possess it for ever and ever. To this period in the prophetic record, the author has given a concise interpretation; which he does not offer as sufficient in itself, (for the revelation is upon that grand and ample scale, that none can ever exhaust the comprehensive subject,) but rather as a guide for the students of this most blessed book; in order, if possible, to assist them in further research for its hidden treasures. To those who have been so far enlightened by the Spirit of truth, as to have overcome the prejudice which is too prevalent against the study of this prophecy, nothing need be offered as incitements to its perusal; but to those who are still labouring under this delusion of Satan, it may be as well to observe, that such can have little conception of the rich profusion of Divine treasure which is couched under this symbolical prophecy; both as affording abundant sources of consolation to himself,

(as composing one of the complete body of Christ,) and likewise
as containing in its ample folds deep openings of Divine truth,
scattered like gems throughout the whole. Such an exuberant
collection of magnificent truths, and conveyed in such splendid
imagery, is no where else to be found ; so truly does that blessing of our Lord, to whom the revelation was first given, and
then bequeathed to his Church, descend upon the diligent and
reverent inquirer into these holy mysteries. "Blessed is he
that readeth, and they that hear the words of this prophecy,
and keep those things which are written therein : for the time
is at hand." (chap. i. 3.)

It will be necessary to offer a few remarks on the internal
structure of the book, and likewise upon the nature of symbolic
prophecy.

It has been laid down by an eminent commentator,* that a
symbolical prophecy should be studied solely with respect to the
symbols, and the structure of the book thus first ascertained
from internal sources, previously to any attempt being made at
an interpretation ; and the strict observance of this most important rule is the only effectual preventative to the encroachment
of fanciful interpretations.

The character of symbolical prophecy necessarily affords a
larger scope to the interpreter than the more literal ; because it
is not found difficult to mould events so as they shall assume, in
some one respect or other, an apparent assimilation to the prophecy ; and thus a spurious interpretation has doubtless often
been presented to the church. Before any interpreter, therefore,
commences his arduous task of explaining symbolical prophecy,
he should take good heed to confine his researches within such
limits as the prophecy itself will not fail to present, when its
structure and arrangement is determined from the symbols
themselves. Acting upon this invaluable and only safe course
to be pursued, Mr. Frere† has rendered a service to the church

* Mede.

† The author cannot omit expressing to this gentleman, his own sense of
obligation for the benefit and instruction he has received from the "Combined View of the Prophecies of Daniel and St. John ;" and also from a
small pamphlet since published, entitled, "On the general Structure of
the Apocalypse, being a brief Introduction to the minute Interpretation."
From both of these works he has received much information necessary to
the arrangement of this interpretation.

which she can scarcely ever repay, by establishing the structure
of this Apocalypse upon a basis of truth which nothing has ever
shaken ; and the interpretation which naturally flows in upon the
erection of such a frame-work is the best proof of its accuracy ;
for that book, which formerly was considered enveloped in mys-
ticism and obscurity, will appear to those who study it upon
that gentleman's scheme, to be a body of heavenly light scarcely
less characterised by the capacity and distinctness it casts upon
every other part of Scripture, than by the simplicity and beauty
of the interpretation to which it conducts.   The author refers
the reader to the pamphlet, entitled, "On the general Structure
of the Apocalypse, being a brief Introduction to its minute Interpretation, by James Hatley Frere, Esq.," which he would
recommend to his most diligent and attentive perusal.   He will,
however, avail himself of an extract, as compressing in a short
compass the arrangement of the prophecy, referring the reader
to the pamphlet itself for the arguments upon which it is founded.

TABLE OF THE CONTENTS OF THE APOCALYPSE.

Chap. I. contains, in verses 1—9, a general introduction, or preface ; and in verses 10—18, a vision of our Lord Jesus Christ,
referred to in chap. i. 19, by the words, "Write the things
which thou hast seen."

Chaps. II, III. consist of the epistles to the seven churches
which are in Asia, described in the same verse (chap. i. 19)
as relating to " the things which are."

The remainder of the Revelation consists of the prophetic his_
tory of future events described in the same verse (chap. i. 19)
as " the things which shall be hereafter," and contains as under, namely.

Chaps. IV. V. VI. VII.—The communication by the cherubic
voices, of the history of the Western Roman Empire ; chaps.
IV. and V. being prefatory.

Chaps. VIII. IX, X. 1—7.—The communication by the voices of
trumpet angels, or the history of the Eastern Roman Empire ;
chap. viii. 1—6, being prefatory.

Chap. X. 8, to the end, and chap. XI.—The first part of the little
open book, communicated by " the voice from heaven," or the

history of the church in brief; chap. x. 8—11 being prefatory.

Chaps. XII. XIII. and XIV.—The remainder of the little open book, communicated by "the voice from heaven," repeating the church history at large, or in the details of its three successive periods.

Chaps. XV. XVI.—The supplementary history, containing the account of the pouring out of the seven golden bowls or vials of wrath, which are common to the last period of the three preceding histories.

Chaps. XVII. XVIII. XIX. 1—10.—The explanation of the angel relative to the first history, namely, that of the Western Roman Empire, announced by the cherubic voices.

Chap. XIX. 11 to the end, XX. XXI. 1—8.—The explanation of the angel relative to the second history, namely, that of the Eastern Roman Empire, announced by the voices of the seven trumpets.

Chap. XXI. 9, to the end, and XXII.—The explanation of the angel relative to the third history ; namely, that of the church announced by " the voice from heaven," and contained in the little open book.

The author has one observation to make upon the nature of symbolical language in general. Whilst this mode of instruction is the most comprehensive and durable, it is likewise the most simple and natural. It is the universal language of mankind ; the heavenly method of teaching man truth ; for natural words will not express spiritual things. Thus it is written in the xixth Psalm, "The heavens declare the glory of God ; and the firmament sheweth his handywork. Day unto day uttereth speech, and night unto night sheweth knowledge. There is no speech nor language, where their voice is not heard." The same truth, that the visible creation is to be regarded as setting forth the invisible, is declared by the Apostle Paul, in his Epistle to the Romans, i. 20 : "For the invisible things of him from the creation of the world are clearly seen, being understood by the things that are made, even his eternal power and Godhead." This is the true character of symbolical language ; the whole world is one great symbol, the perfection of the Deity

seen and known in all his visible works : this is the sublime
origin of all symbols, and the only true method of arriving to
the knowledge of any deep truths in the spiritual and invisible
world. We are hereby furnished with an argument in favour of
the truth of our holy religion, in contradistinction to that of the
surrounding impostures of the heathen nations ; for if the hidden
mysteries of our religion are found enclosed in the fold of the visible creation, who could be the originator of that religion but the
Creator himself? For he alone who from chaos produced this
world of light, and life, and beauty, could shape things seen so as
to represent and shadow forth things unseen : who can know
the hidden mysteries of nature—but nature's Lord ?

As an illustration of the comprehensiveness of the symbolic
language, the sun and moon may be instanced, which the reader
will recognize as continually alluded to in Scripture, as symbolical of the Sun of Righteousness, even Christ : and the moon,
as emblematical of his church, his chaste spouse. By an accur-
ate examination of the natural fact, and comparing it with the
thing signified, it will be seen with what exactness the one
shadows forth the other. The sun (as far as it respects our
planetary system) is an independent body of light : so is Christ
the source of all spiritual blessing to his church. The moon is in
herself an opaque body : so the church has neither form nor
comeliness, and possesses no beauty in herself, but as she derives
it from the imputed righteousness of Christ ; and being clothed
with which, she sheds her borrowed lustre upon a world lying
beneath her, in darkness and in error. The sun's rays are hid
from that portion of the earth, which is immersed in the darkness of night, and is apparently all unconscious of his existence
—not so the moon, who still enjoys the full blaze of his efful-
gent brightness. Thus the true church can by faith recognize
and enjoy the presence of her Lord, and receive that consolation and support from the light of his countenance, of which a
world, lying in wickedness, is wholly ignorant. The similarity
might be carried to a greater extent, but this probably will suf-
fice, as an example of the fulness of the symbolical style.

The author has annexed a short symbolical dictionary, in
order to obviate the impression that the interpretation of the
symbols is arbitrarily assumed, and likewise to assist the student

of this interesting prophecy.   It is an abbreviated extract from
Mr. Frere's " Combined View of the Prophecies ;" to which the
reader is directed for a more enlarged explanation

The Earth	The territories which were the seat of the four great empires.
The third part of the Earth	The Eastern Roman Empire, of which Constantinople was the capital, being that portion which fell to Constantine, on the division of the empire by Constantine the Great, among his three sons.
The fourth part of the Earth	Italy, together with the Roman Province of Africa, being one of the four prefectures into which the Roman Empire was divided by Constantine the Great. (Rev. vi. 8.)
An Earthquake	A popular commotion, threatening the overthrow of a kingdom.
Sun	The Lord of day, in temporals, the King ; spiritually, the Sun of Righteousness ; Christ.
Moon	The Queen of heaven ; the consort of the sun, the queen ; spiritually, the church.
Stars	The princes and nobles of a kingdom ; spiritually apostles or ministers of the church.
Heavens	The political system of government, in which these symbolical planets appear.
Great Waters	Multitudes of people. The noise of many waters is as the noise of a multitude of people.
Sea	" The untillable and barren deep," peoples in an unfruitful state, subject to storm, &c.
Sea of Glass	Population in a tranquil state.
Four Winds	The spirit of violence and discord, which when let loose acts on the sea, or population.
River Euphrates	The Turkish Empire, which first rose in the neighbourhood of that river.
Air	Descriptive of universality.
Beasts	Savage, indicate political brutal power ; beasts of Rev., various significations, Infidel power and Papacy.
Heads of a Beast ...	The rulers of a kingdom or empire.
Chaste Woman	Spouse of Christ, the true church, bringing forth spiritual children.

Unchaste Woman...	The great harlot, the Papacy, who induce kings of the earth to commit fornication.
Fornication........	Spiritual Idolatry.
Kings of the Earth..	The rulers of the Papal nations.
Babylon...........	The Papacy and its adherents.
Holy City, Jerusalem	Used symbolically of the present visible church literally that city which comes down from God.
Temple............	Holy of holies symbolizes heavenly things, the New Jerusalem the presence of God. Holy place symbolizes the spiritual church on earth, the true priesthood. Outer court symbolizes professors of religion only, not spiritual worshippers.
Living Creatures...	The church, taken from the four banners of Judah, Ephraim, Reuben, and Dan, who usually encamped around the tabernacle.
Incense, or Sweet Odours	The prayers of saints.
White Robes.......	The righteousness of Christ.
Rain	The Holy Spirit.
Grass.............	True believers flourishing under the waters of the Spirit of God.
Rivers and Fountains	Sources of religious instruction.
Flood of Waters....	A large body of men, an army in motion.
Storm of Hail......	Northern armies, where hail is supposed to generate.
Flight of Locusts...	Southern armies, whence locusts came.
Ships.............	Establishments of those who make a gain of godliness.
Shipmaster, or Merchants.........	Venal Ecclesiastics.
Wings	Emblematical of swiftness.
Horse.............	Emblematical of power and authority.
Tail of Scorpion...	Seat of poison—false and deadly doctrines.
Prophetic Day.....	A year.
Month	30 years.
Time	360 years.
Half a Time.......	180 years.
Prophetic Hour....	A month, or twelfth part of a year, a short period.
Harvest of Mercy...	Protection and ingathering of the saints.
Harvest of Wrath..	Act of judgment.
Vintage, or Treading Wine-press.	Last act of judgment after the harvest.
Fire	Destruction inflicted upon an enemy.
Lightning	Fire from heaven, a manifest act of vengeance.

| Voice of Thunder, or Voice of Trumpet. | Voice of the church in heaven, and declaration of God's judgement on his enemies. |

It now only remains for the author to acknowledge the deep debt of gratitude he owes to the Rev. Edward Irving, to whose exposition of the Apocalypse, delivered at the Scotch Church, during the year 1828, he is chiefly indebted for the interpretation of the prophetical parts of the book, and whose enlightened ministry he must regard as instrumental to his attainments of any theological truths contained in this commentary. He has not deemed it requisite to state such authority in the body of the work, in the very many instances, wherein the ideas are presented almost as genuine as they proceeded from him, because the work would have abounded with a too-frequent repetition of such acknowledgments, seeing that he has arrived to the understanding of almost every Divine truth by instructions received from the lips of his respected pastor. This acknowledgment is offered to the public, rather in compliance with the maxims of this world's wisdom, than to be regarded as the expression of his own obligations; for they are of too sacred a character to admit of their allusion in terms of common courtesy.

The author has one observation to offer for the consideration of the reader, previously to closing these few preliminary remarks; and in this, a careless reader will peruse this book, and derive as little benefit as though he never read it: but let him attentively compare the interpretation offered, with the text, making every adequate allowance for the essential difference between a symbol and an historical fact, the sign and the thing signified, and by the blessing of God he may not only become a wiser but a better man; for, assuredly, the blessing rests upon him who "readeth, and they that hear the words of this prophecy."

Into the hands of Almighty God the Author commits this feeble attempt to make known the truths contained in this holy prophecy, praying that he will graciously pardon the many imperfections it contains, and also if he has unknowingly and heedlessly "added unto these things, or taken any away from the words of the book of this prophecy," that the punishment threatened against such may not alight on his head, seeing that he hath done it in ignorance; but rather that his name may be found written in the Book of Life, and that he may have inheritance in that holy city which cometh down out of heaven from his God, for Christ's sake. *Amen.*

London, May, 8, 1829.

CHAPTER I.

This first chapter comprises the things which the Apostle *had seen* (v. 19), and which he was told by our Lord to write. The most enlarged and comprehensive views of the mysterious doctrine of the blessed Trinity will be found contained in it, with the various offices and character of the Persons in the Godhead.

This book is justly entitled the Revelation of Jesus Christ, both because it contains a prophetic communication made by God the Father to Jesus Christ, in virtue of his resurrection as Son of Man (see Mark xiii. 32); and more especially because its ultimate object is the glorious coming of Jesus Christ, to redeem his suffering church, avenge her oppressors, and establish in everlasting power his own kingdom on earth, on the ruins of the antichristian kings. The Angel through whom it was communicated to John, was one of the church in heaven. (See xix. 10; xxii. 9; v. 10.)

1 The Revelation of Jesus Christ, which God gave unto him, to shew unto his servants things which must shortly come to pass; and he sent and signified it by his angel unto his servant John:

"He that is faithful in that which is least, is faithful also in much." The beloved disciple, who bare the "true record" of Christ's humility (John xix. 35), was selected as the witness of his majesty and glory.

2 Who bare record of the word of God, and of the testimony of Jesus Christ, and of all things that he saw.

There can scarcely exist a more animating encouragement to the study and continual observance of the things declared in this most holy prophecy, than is contained in this verse; such a manifest incitement to its perusal being found attached to no other prophecy in the inspired Volume; and which, coupled with the instruction to the Apostle (xxii. 10), "Seal

3 Blessed is he that readeth, and they that hear the words of this prophecy, and keep those things which are written therein: for the time is at hand.

B

not the sayings of the prophecy of this book," distinctly and unequivocally notifies to the church, that the mysteries therein contained were never designed by its Divine Author to be sealed to them : but, though it foretold them of the " much tribulation through which they were to enter into the kingdom of God," yet likewise spake of a redemption and of an inheritance " near at hand."

4 John to the seven churches which are in Asia : Grace be unto you, and peace, from Him which is, and which was, and which is to come ; and from the seven Spirits which are before his throne.

5 And from Jesus Christ, who is the faithful witness, and the first-begotten of the dead, and the Prince of the kings of the earth. Unto him that loved us, and washed us from our sins in his own blood ;

6 And hath made us kings and priests unto God and his Father ; to him be glory and dominion for ever and ever. Amen.

This Revelation is addressed to seven churches of the Eastern Empire, which has the precedence, inasmuch as it was so long the chief seat of the church, was the principal theatre of Christ's suffering and humility, and is hereafter to be the spot upon which his glory will be more strikingly manifested. Seven churches are addressed, as representing the whole ; the number seven being indicative of totality, or perfection. The benediction is that of the ever-blessed Trinity ; the seven spirits characterizing the Holy Ghost, not so much in his eternal subsistence, as in his diffusive and illuminating influence extended over the churches, proceeding from the Son of Man, who sitteth on the throne. " The Prince of the kings of the earth" is Christ's true and proper title ; to the investiture in which dignity this prophecy most especially refers ; and in the participation of which kingly power he will instal all those who have been " washed from their sins in his own blood," and will make them kings and priests unto God and his Father, when he shall give the kingdom to the saints of the Most High, who shall possess it for ever, even for ever and ever. Amen.

7 Behold, he cometh with clouds, and every eye shall see him, and they also which pierced him : and all kin-

The future glorious revelation of Jesus Christ is here set forth as the great object of the prophecy, being the grand and momentous event which all the various dispensations of God's providence, revealed therein, in the Divine plan are designed to accelerate, and in which they shall all terminate; the latter part of the verse clearly denoting the terrific judgments with which he will visit the nations of the earth at his advent.

This is a commencing as well as a terminating text (xxi. 6, and xxii. 13), setting forth the power and Godhead of Christ, who is the author of the prophecy. The same characteristic being applied to the First Person in the Trinity in verse 4, declares his equality and oneness with the Father.

St. John here introduces himself as the accredited agent of communicating to the church this consolatory prophecy; and begins by stating his qualification for the office, in having participated in the trials and suffering of the saints, in the patient endurance of which the Apostle found there was great reward.

The day of the resurrection was most appropriately chosen by our Lord for the abundant outpouring of his Spirit on the Apostle, to prepare him for the important service in which he was about to be employed. The similitude of a voice, as of thunder, or a trumpet, expressive of sublimity and abruptness, is the voice of the church which ought ever to be regarded with fear and reverence. (See chap. iv. 1; viii. 13; xiv. 2).

The Apostle is here commanded to write those revelations in a book which were about to be communicated to him; signifying that the application and use was not confined to the seven churches to whom they

dreds of the earth shall wail because of him. Even so, Amen.

8 I am Alpha and Omega, the beginning and the ending, saith the Lord, which is, and which was, and which is to come, the Almighty.

9 I, John, who also am your brother and companion in tribulation, and in the kingdom and patience of Jesus Christ, was in the isle that is called Patmos, for the word of God, and for the testimony of Jesus Christ.

10 I was in the Spirit on the Lord's-day, and heard behind me a great voice, as of a trumpet.

11 Saying, I am Alpha and Omega, the first and the last: and what thou seest, write in a book, and send it unto the seven churches which are in Asia unto *Ephesus,* and unto *Smyrna, and unto Pergamos, and unto* Thyatira, and unto Sardis, *and unto* Philadelphia, *and unto* Laodicea. were particularly addressed, but, like the Epistles, (many of which were likewise directed to separate churches), they were intended for the church universal, until the end of time : which view of the extended reference of all these Epistles is confirmed chap. ii. 25, wherein the church at Thyatira is directed to "hold that fast which she had till Christ come."

12 *And I turned to see the voice that spake with me. And being turned, I saw seven golden candlesticks, (the visible churches).—* The seven golden candlesticks allude to the candlestick with six branches and seven lamps in the tabernacle (Exod. xxv. 31—37), the candlestick being the sustainer and container of the seven lamps which were constantly kept burning in the tabernacle ; and which we find, from chap. iv. 5, denoted the Spirit of God, the Light of the world, to be found alone in the true visible church : which interpretation of the emblematical character of the candlesticks our Lord himself condescends to give the Apostle. (see verse 20).

13 *And in the midst of the seven candlesitcks, one like unto the Son of Man, clothed with a garment* (priestly) *down to the foot and girt about the paps with a golden girdle* (kingly). Christ is here represented as arrayed in his priestly robes, as the Son of Man, walking amongst and watching over his churches ; the golden girdle being also significant of his kingly character. The figure is aptly expressive of this proximity to his church during persecution or affliction ; for we likewise read that one like the son of Man was seen walking with the three children of Israel in the fiery furnace, and delivered them from the flames.

14. *His head and his hairs were* white like *wool, as* white *as snow,* and his *eyes were as a flame of fire :* This description coincides with that of the Ancient of Days in Daniel, affording one of the many evidences that every revelation made to us of God the Father is of God in Christ. His eyes being like a flame of fire, indicate his discernment of the thoughts and intents of the heart ; as when on earth he needed not that any should testify of man, for he knew what was in man.

This figure of feet like unto fine brass, we find on the like occasions in visions of Jesus Christ—as Ezek. i. 7; Dan. x. 6—used only as descriptive of the Son of Man, and seems to point out the unrelenting character of those judgments, when he will tread the winepress of the wrath of Almighty God. His voice, as the sound of many waters, is applied to the living creatures in Ezek. i. 24, and to the cherubim in Rev. xiv. 2; the former, emblematical of the church in heaven; the latter, of the church on earth.

15 And his feet like unto fine brass, as if they burned in a furnace, and his voice as the sound of many waters

Christ himself interprets this symbol (v. 20) to be the seven angels or ministers of the churches; and his holding them in his right hand, conveys the same encouraging truth as when he declared of his sheep that none should ever pluck them out of his hand. The sword going forth from his mouth, has reference to the great and dreadful judgment, which, as the sword of God, he will execute upon his enemies and the enemies of his church in the last days. (chap. xix. 21.) His countenance shining as the sun, corresponds with his appearance when he manifested himself to St. Paul, as well as at the transfiguration, which were both typical of his future glorious appearance.

16 And he had in his right hand seven stars (the ministers of the churches) and out of his mouth went a sharp two-edged sword (ch. xix. 21), and his countenance was as the sun shineth in his strength.

The Apostle, being, like the Prophet Daniel, struck down with awe at the heavenly vision, is encouraged by Christ laying his right hand upon him; as in that instance the prophet was strenghtened. And by his declaration, that He it was that was dead, and yet liveth, he conveyed the important truth to St. John, that "to him belonged the issues from death" (Psa. lxviii. 29), and that he possessed the keys of the first and of the second death. (Rev. xx. 14.)

17 And when I saw him I fell at his feet as dead. And he laid his right hand upon me, saying unto me, Fear not; I am the first and the last:

18 I am he that liveth, and was dead; and, behold I am alive for evermore, Amen: and have the keys of hell and of death.

The revelation is here divided into

19 Write the things which

thou hast seen and the things which are, and the things which shall be hereafter: three distinct parts: first, The glorious vision which the Apostle had just seen; second, The things which are, consisting of the Epistles to the seven churches (chap. ii. and iii.) exhorting them to patience and faithfulness during the period of the Pagan persecutions, under which they were then suffering; and, third, The things which shall be hereafter, commencing at chap. iv. and containing the three descriptions of persecutions through which the church would have to pass—the Pagan, the Papal, and the Infidel—and thus following the history of the church, until Christ her Head, should himself appear for her deliverance.

20 *The mystery of the seven stars which thou sawest in my right hand, and the seven golden candlesticks. The seven stars, are the angles of the seven churches; and the seven candlesticks which thou sawest, are the seven churches.* Christ here explains the meaning of the vision, as in Dan. xii. 7; thereby confirming the accuracy of the symbol of the candlesticks as more fully interpreted, verse 12, and that of the stars in our comment, on verse 16. With such Divine authority for our guide, there can exist little danger of an erroneous interpretation of these symbols, so often occurring in the prophetic writings.

The second and third chapters comprise the things *which are* (i. 19), and present our Lord in the character of universal Bishop of his Church.

EPHESUS was one of the most splendid cities of Asia Minor, being remarkable for its opulence, its voluptuousness, and its idolatry ; and was considered the metropolis of all Asia. The church of Ephesus was planted by St. Paul, and afterwards transferred to the charge of Timothy : St. John also ministered in it after his return from Patmos. Christ addresses individually the ministers of the churches, communicating through them to their people : and by commending them when their flocks are distinguished for faithfulness, or by reproving them when they have forsaken the faith, it is evident the great Head of the church considers his ministers representative of, and responsible for, the spiritual condition of their respective charges. There is a uniform consistency and peculiar propriety in these epistles, which it is most necessary to keep in view ; and which preliminary observations will strictly apply to each separate address. The Divine Author of these epistles announces his authority and headship over the churches, by a reference to the sublime vision of him-

1. *Unto the angel of the church of Ephesus write ; These things saith he that holdeth the seven stars in his right hand, who walketh in the midst of the seven golden candlesticks.*

2 *I know thy works, and thy labour, and thy patience and how thou canst not bear them which are evil ; and thou hast tried them which say they are apostles, and are not, and hast found them liars.*

3. *And hast borne, and hast patience, and for my name's sake hast laboured, and hast not fainted.*

4 *Nevertheless I have somewhat against thee, because thou hast left thy first love.*

5. *Remember therefore from whence thou art fallen, and repent, and do the first works ; or else I will come unto thee quickly, and will remove thy candlestick out of his place, except thou repent.*

6. But this thou hast, that thou hatest the deeds of the Nicolaitans, which I also hate.

7. He that hath an ear, let him hear what the Spirit saith unto the churches: To him that overcometh will I give to eat of the tree of life, which is in the midst of the paradise of God.

self, which he had just exhibited to his faithful Apostle: and as the superscription is different to each church, St. John's description of the vision is divided for this purpose into seven parts. The address is a commentary on the superscription; or rather the latter is selected as a motto indicative of the religious state of the church. The encouraging promise with which each address terminates, will be likewise found peculiarly adapted to revive the courage and strengthen the hopes of the church whose spiritual condition is the subject of address, and its universality of application, and right of appropriation to all ages of the church of Christ, until his second coming is placed beyond all question, by each promise being scrupulously introduced in every instance, announcing its propriety to "all that overcome;" and by the concluding declaration that its blessings comprehend encouragements to all "that have an ear." The promises likewise contained in each address, all refer to a period of blessedness subsequent to the Lord's coming, to be enjoyed in the New Jerusalem condition of the church; which was consequently to be considered as an object of the church's expectation, *until he came.* The promise to him that overcometh, held out to the church of Ephesus, of the "tree of life," in the paradise of God, is pregnant with important meaning; and is found twice referred to, in the description of the millennial state, in the last two chapters of this book. (chap. xxii. 2, 14.) The paradise contained in the first chapters of Genesis, is but the type of the paradise of the last two chapters of the Apocalypse; the former the generation, the latter the regeneration of all things; the inspired volume thus exhibiting, according to the Jewish notion in the space of a week of seven thousand years, the original creation, subsequent fall, and final restitution of all things. In the first paradise, Adam was fully invested with dominion and lordship over all things (Gen. i. 26); the tree of life in the garden, and Eve taken from his bleeding side. In the second paradise, Christ, the second Adam, the Lord from heaven, whose power extends to all things both in heaven and earth, to principalities and powers (Heb. ii. compared with Psa. viii.) ; and joining with him in this universal sway his faithful spouse, the church, likewise (in the figure) taken from his side. In both, there is the tree of life ; but inasmuch as in the former it was prohibited, and in the latter, the regeneration, a participation thereof is held out as a high reward, the conclusion is obvious from this, as from every other particular narrated, that the paradise of which Christ is the head will as far transcend that of Adam in magnitude and glory, as the character and attributes of Him who will re-constitute and in himself sustain all things, was superior to his through whose defection the dominion of the world, and man's eminence in the scale of God's creatures, was lost. There is a hidden signification in the act of eating, which we seem little disposed to attach to it. It is the outward symbol, chosen by our Lord, to set forth one of the deepest mysteries of our holy religion, the believer's participation of his body and blood. It was made the test of obedience to our first parents ; by which tenure they held their ample dominion ; but failing in this, and eating of the forbidden fruit, we learn consequent upon that act, their instant moral recognition of good and evil. (Gen. iii. 22.) It was God's solicitude lest they should likewise put forth their hand and take also of the tree of life and live for ever, that induced him, in mercy, to banish them from the garden of Eden. We see, therefore, from analogy, every reason to conclude that high and eternal spiritual benefits may be intimately associated with the outward act of participation of the tree of life in the paradise of God, promised to the faithful of the church of Ephesus. They, however, took not Christ's warning, and the candlestick is removed ; Ephesus is now a heap of ruins, containing a few wretched inhabitants and no church.

.Smyrna, in the time of the Apostles, was considered the second city in Asia. As the church at Smyrna was in tribulation and poverty, and was furthermore to undergo severe persecutions, Christ announces himself as the First and the Last, which was dead and is alive again ; and

8 *And unto the angel of the church in Smyrna write ; These things saith the first and the last, which was dead, and is alive :*

9 *I know thy works, and tribulation, and poverty, (but thou art rich) and I*

know the blasphemy of them *which* **say** they are Jews, and **are not, but are the synagogue of Satan.**

10 *Fear none of those things which thou shalt suffer; behold, the devil shall cast some of you into prison, that ye may be tried; and ye shall have tribulation ten days; be thou faithful unto death, and I will give thee a crown of life.*

11 *He that hath an ear, let him hear what the spirit saith unto the churches: He that overcometh shall not be hurt of the second death.*

encourages them to fear none of those things which they should suffer, by the animating assurance that he, their Lord and Head, had also suffered death; through which he destroyed him that had the power of death, that is, the devil; and by his resurrection had acquired victory over him. We may here learn, by the commendations which Christ bestows on the church at Smyrna, not only that affliction and poverty are favourable to the advance of true spirituality, the saints being perfected through sufferings, even as Christ himself was (Heb. ii. 10), but, from comparison with the other churches, who are represented in more prosperous conditions, we may fairly infer, that such is absolutely necessary to a continuance of growth in grace. Satan is here pointed out as the great instigator of all persecutions, acting in his true character, as accuser of the brethren. The ten days, more particularly referred to, in all probability allude to the final persecution under Dioclesian and his successors, which is always described by the ancient writers as the Ten-Years' Persecution.* As the church of Smyrna, to purify her faith, was destined to the fiery ordeal of death, she is incited to its patient endurance by the hope of a crown of life, which, St. Paul informs us, the Lord the righteous judge shall give unto all that fight the good fight, and keep the faith, in that day of his appearing (2 Tim. iv. 7, 8); which we know, from chap. xix. 11—21 to be immediately preceding the establishment of Christ's millennial reign. If they overcome, and endure unto the end, they shall be made participators in the first resurrection, on whom the second death hath no power. (chap. xx. 6—14; xxi. 8).

* See Milner's Church History, vol. ii. p. 4; also Cave's Introduction to Lives of the Fathers: in which the Pagan persecutions are divided into ten acts, the last of which continued ten years; beginning in the reign of Dioclesian, Feb. 23, 303, and terminating in that of Constantine, A. D. 321.

Smyrna still continues a chief commercial city of the Levant, and contains in her a Christian church.

Pergamos, the ancient capital of the line of Attalus, was celebrated for its literature and libertinism, its philosophy and its magnificence; and therefore it is said, "even where Satan's seat is." Riches, and their accompaniments, ever have been a powerful engine in Satan's hands to destroy the church. The minister is commended for holding fast the faith, surrounded with such combinations to infidelity: whilst, on the other hand, he is reproved for laxity of discipline, in not visiting with judicial excommunication those who held the doctrines of Balaam, and of the Nicolaitanes. Christ therefore, announces himself as He who hath the sharp sword with two edges (chap. xix. 15—21), with which he executes judgment; and threatens, unless they repent, he will fight against them with the sword of his mouth, and deal to them that righteous judgment, which, from a principle of expediency and accommodation, they neglected to observe towards these heresies. The doctrine of Balaam was to corrupt, not so much by outward opposition, as by holding out inducements to commit sin; even as that prophet, by listening to and temporising with Balac the king of Moab, occasioned that forbidden intercourse with the Moabitish women, which speedily led to an adoption of their idolatrous worship. Of the Nicolaitanes little

12 *And to the angel of the church in Pergamos write; These things saith he which hath the sharp sword with two edges:*

13 *I know thy works, and where thou dwellest, even where Satan's seat is; and thou holdest fast my name, and hast not denied my faith, even in those days wherein Antipas was my faithful martyr, who was slain among you, where Satan dwelleth.*

14. *But I have a few things against thee, because thou hast there them that hold the doctrine of Balaam, who taught Balac to cast a stumbling-block before the children of Israel, to eat things sacrificed unto idols, and to commit fornication.*

15 *So hast thou also them that hold the doctrine of the Nicolaitanes, which thing I hate.*

16 *Repent; or else I will come unto thee quickly, and will fight against them with the sword of my mouth.*

17 *He that hath an ear, let him hear what the Spirit saith unto the churches: To him that*

*overcometh will **I give to*** *eat of the hidden manna,* *and will give him a white* *stone, **and in the stone a*** *new name written, which* *no man knoweth saving **he*** *that receiveth it.* is known. Commentators have not been able to acquire authentic information. Scott says it was the Antinomian heresy. But of this we may be satisfied, **from the** mention of it in another church, that it was **at that** period a prevailing error, **which pe-** culiarly attracted the indignation of our Lord. To those who overcome is promised the hidden manna. "I am the bread of life," says Christ (John vi.): "whoso eateth my flesh and drinketh my blood hath eternal life. Not as your fathers did eat manna, and are dead : he that eateth of this bread shall live for ever." The bread of life, even Christ, is now hid from our sight ; but hereafter to be revealed at his second coming.— They shall likewise have a white stone ; and in the stone a new name written, which no man knoweth saving he that receiveth it. The white stone refers to the mode of acquittal adopted by the Areopagus, and indicates the first resurrection, which shall declare those who partake in it to be the sons of God with power. " Who shall lay anything to the charge of God's elect ?" Christ is represented, chap. xix. 12 (which contains a **most** sublime description of his second advent), to have on that occasion a new name written, that no man knew, but he himself : no doubt referring to the same mystery contained in the promise to the church of Pergamos.

Pergamos still continues in existence in Asiatic Turkey, the Christian population amounting to about 3000.

18 *And unto the angel of the church in Thyatira write ; These things saith the Son of God, who hath his eyes like unto a flame of fire, and his feet are like fine brass ;* Thyatira **was a considerable city in** Asia, **and** is mentioned in **Acts xvi.** 14, as the residence of **Lydia.** The declaration of **Christ in** the super- scription, that he is the Son of God, is peculiar **to** this address ; **and the** reason is, doubtless, because the con- cluding promise refers to that domi- nion he is to have over the nations of the earth, and which he will exercise by delegating that power to his risen saints (**Ps. ii.** 9 ; chap. xix. 15.) **His**

19 *I know thy works, and* **charity, and service,** and *faith, and thy patience, and* **thy** works **; and** the last to *be more **than the first.***

eyes like unto a flame of fire, denote the penetration with which he searcheth the heart and reins (ver. 23); and his feet like fine brass (Dan. x. 6) signify the unrelenting severity of those judgments, spoken of in Micah iv. 12, when he shall gather together the nations as the sheaves into the floor, and trample upon many people, as with horns of iron and hoofs of brass. The symbol describes the character of that dominion of the Son of God prophesied of in the 110th Psalm—and participation of which is held out as a great object of hope to the church at Thyatira (ver. 26, 27)— when he shall strike through kings in the day of his wrath, and rule his enemies with a rod of iron. After enumerating wherein the minister of the church had shewn stability and spiritual improvement, Christ proceeds to acquaint him that he has something against him. The defection appears to consist in not counteracting the heretical opinions of a certain woman, who is here represented allegorically as Jezebel the wife of Ahab, who kept four hundred idol prophets at her table, and exerted all her influence to promote idolatry. Adultery, and similar expressions, when used of a church, invariably mean a declension of true religion and adherence to a false one: and those who had given way to this temptation, are threatened with a bed of infirmity, sickness, and death, unless they speedily repent of

20 *Notwithstanding, I have a few things against thee, because thou sufferest that woman Jezebel, which calleth herself a prophetess to teach and to seduce my servants to commit fornication, and to eat things sacrificed unto idols.*

21 *And I gave her space to repent of her fornication, and she repented not.*

22 *Behold I will cast her into a bed, and them that commit adultery with her into great tribulation, except they repent of their deeds.*

23 *And I will kill her children with death and all the churches shall know that I am he which searcheth the reins and hearts; and I will give unto every one of you according to your works.*

24 *But unto you I say, and unto the rest in Thyatira, as many as have not this doctrine, and which have not known the depths of Satan, as they speak; I will put upon you none other burden.*

25 *But that which ye have already hold fast till I come.*

26 *And he that overcometh, and keepeth my*

works unto the end, to him will I give power over the nations:

27 And he shall rule them with a rod of Iron ; as the vessels of a potter shall they be broken to shivers ; even as I received of my Father.

28 And I will give him the morning star.

29. He that hath an ear, let him hear what the Spirit saith unto the churches.

their deeds. We may learn, from the great importance that our great Head attaches to purity of doctrine, in this and the epistle to the angel at Pergamos, that any defection in this respect is the first step towards complete apostasy from the truth. Those who are exempt from this form of heresy in the church at Thyatira, are encouraged to hold that fast until Christ comes (ver. 25): which expression affords us additional proof that the exhortations and promises, contained in these epistles, were intended for general application until that event. The " morning star " is the first resurrection (Ps. xlix. 14, &c.); and, being taken in connection with the expression in the 25th verse, "till I come," indicates that those who are faithful shall then receive that better resurrection from Him " to whom belongeth the issues from death," who is himself the root and offspring of David, and the bright and morning-star (chap. xxii. 16).

Thyatira still exists—but the church repented not ; the threatenings were fulfilled against her ; and no vestige of a church remains.

CHAP. III.—1 .And unto the angel of the church in Sardis write ; These things saith he that hath the seven Spirits of God, and the seven stars ; I know thy works, that thou hast a name that thou livest, and art dead.

2. Be watchful, and strengthen the things which remain, that are ready to die, for I have not found thy works perfect before God.

3 Remember therefore how

SARDIS was the ancient seat of the Lydian Kings, and memorable as the city of Crœsus. It was, like the chief cities of Asia, magnificent, intellectual, and profligate. In the epistle to the church of Ephesus, Christ is said to hold the seven stars in his right hand ; but here he claims " to have " the seven Spirits of God, and the seven stars. The seven Spirits of God (see chap. v. 6,) is the Holy Ghost, as proceeding from the Father through the humanity of Christ : the figure here represents him as the great dispenser of the Spirit to his churches: as when he said, "It is expedient for you that I go away; for if I go not away, the Comforter (which is the Holy Ghost) will not come unto you: but if I depart I will send him unto you" (John xvi. 7): see also John xiv. 16, 26, and John xv. 26. The stars or ministers of the churches, are Christ's by special propriety. He asserts his authority over the angel of the church at Sardis, and justifies his right to call him to a strict account of his stewardship. But he was negligent and faithless in the discharge of that high office, with which he had been invested by the great Bishop; for we are informed he had, "a name to live, whilst he was dead." He was like a tree dead at the root, having a shew of life in the leaf. Yet not beyond recovery; and he is therefore urged to be watchful, and

thou hast received and heard, and hold fast, and repent. If therefore thou shalt not watch, I will come on thee as a thief, and thou shalt not know what hour I will come upon thee.

4 Thou hast a few names even in Sardis which have not defiled their garments, and they shall walk with me in white; for they are worthy.

5 He that overcometh, the same shall be clothed in white raiment; and I will not blot out his name out of the book of life, but I will confess his name before my Father, and before his angels.

6 He that hath an ear, let him hear what the Spirit saith unto the churches.

to strengthen the things that remain, that were ready to die. But should he continue in such an unprofitable state, Christ threatens to come upon him in judgment, with the suddenness of a thief; and he shall be surprised in the careless condition of those who look not for their Lord's return. It is by the unfaithful alone that Christ's coming is to be regarded with apprehension, for to the church at Philadelphia his speedy approach is held out as an object of encouragement. There were still a few names, even in Sardis: and he promises these shall walk with him in white raiment, the wedding-garment of his own righteousness (vi. 11; vii. 9, 13, 14; and xix. 8) whose names shall be retained in the book of life, and whom the Lamb will acknowledge before his Father and the holy angels.—How pregnant is this epistle with spiritual instruction! Alas! how imperceptibly, yet how fatally, does negligence and worldly-mindedness steal upon our souls, and thus gradually introduces an utter forgetfulness of the higher ends of our being! We have here an awful truth presented to our reflection; that it is possible for a society of persons, all professing godliness, and supporting a consistent reputation in the estimation of men, yet by far the greater majority still to continue in the gall of bitterness and in the bond of iniquity :—though having a name to live in the eyes of their fellow-men, and reposing in such a fallacious dependency, they possibly may be going down to hell with a lie in their right hand. Surely such a state of self-gratulation and security, ought ever to be regarded with suspicion, for it resembles the ominous stillness and fatal ease which ever precedes the dissolution of a corrupt and gangrenous body.

Sardis perished in the general decay of Asia Minor.

7 *And to the angel of the church in Philadelphia write ; These things saith he that is holy, he that is true, he that hath the key of David, he that openeth, and no man shutteth ; and shutteth, and no man openeth :*

8 *I know thy works ; behold, I have set before thee an open door, and no man can shut it ; for thou hast a little strength, and hast kept my word, and hast not denied my name.*

9 *Behold, I will make them of the synagogue of Satan, which say they are Jews, and are not, but do lie ; behold, I will make them to come and worship before thy feet, and to know that I have loved thee.*

Philadelphia had been a flourishing city in Asia, situated by the river Cogamus, twenty-seven miles E. S. E. of Sardis. This is the only instance, in the address of these seven epistles, that the attributes by which Christ announces himself to the angel are not contained, in the express words, in the vision to the Apostle. They are, however, implied ; and each conveys to us a deep and important truth. Christ is the only creature who is holy : he was pronounced holy from his conception, and rose from the dead in virtue of his spotless purity ; being a high priest "holy, harmless, undefiled, and separate from sinners." He was emphatically the True One : John says, chap. i. 17, " the law was given by Moses, but grace and truth came by Jesus Christ." In the person of Jesus Christ the truth was embodied : he who was the source of light to the prophets of old, was now in human form: the Word become flesh. Therefore, he, and he only could say, " I am the truth." (John xiv. 6.)—These things saith " he that hath the key of David." In this expression, Christ is represented as steward of the king's house: probably here introduced to describe his headship over all temporalities, as well as over the churches; and particularly to be regarded as the assertion of his authority over the house of Israel, applicable to those troublesome Jews, whom he threatens to make of the synagogue of Satan, and bring to submission, before the feet of his faithful minister. The angel had been entrusted only with a little power, but he had employed it to the glory of his Master: he had kept his word, and had not denied his name : therefore Christ will keep him from the hour of temptation, which shall come on all the world, to try them. Christ, in inflicting judgment, will ever distinguish be-

10 *Because thou hast kept the word of my patience, I also will keep thee from the hour of temptation, which shall come upon all the world, to try them that dwell upon the earth.*

11 *Behold, I come quickly; hold that fast which thou hast, that no man take thy crown.*

12 *Him that overcometh will I make a pillar in the temple of my God, and he shall go no more out ; and I will write upon him the name of my God, and the name of the city of my God which is new Jerusalem, which cometh down out of heaven from my God : and I will write upon him my new name.*

13 *He that hath an ear, let him hear what the Spirit saith unto the churches.*

tween him who serveth God and him who serveth him not. Patient endurance, and perseverance in faithfulness, cannot fail of reaping their due reward ; for it is those only who endure unto the end that shall be saved. St. Paul presents the same truth as our Lord, in his Epistle to the Galatians, whom he encourages " not to be weary in well-doing for in due season they shall reap, if they faint not :" for there were some among them who did run well for a time, but were hindered. Alas! how large a proportion are there who receive the Gospel with joy, and yet have not sufficient depth of soil to endure trial or temptation! If the Great Bishop had not known the angel of the church at Philadelphia was beset by temptations, the **exhortation would** have been supererogatory, **that he should hold that fast which** he had, that no man might take his **crown.** There is scarcely any injunction so constanly held up to the observance of the Christian, as **constancy** in watchfulness : and surely no condition of mind can be more pregnant with danger than a presumptuous and heedless confidence. The fullest assurance of faith is compatible: nay, it is but an ill-grounded hope if it be unaccompanied with a holy fear. Christ cheers the angel's warfare by the bright expectation of his near approach—which is ever the grand object of the church's hope —for then should he receive a crown of glory, and an inheritance incorruptible, undefiled, and that fadeth not away. The rewards and encouragements held out to him that overcometh in this address to the Philadelphian church, are far larger and more explicit than to any other ; and are all to be found contained in that description of the heavenly city, in the last two chapters of this book.

Philadelphia still exists in Asiatic Turkey, in the town now called Allah-shehr, or Alashehr, which means " The City of God." The number of houses is said to be about three thousand, of which two hundred and fifty are Greek. The Christians have twenty-five places of worship, five of them large and regular churches ; a resident bishop, and twenty inferior clergy.

14 *And unto the angel of the church of the Laodiceans write; these things saith the Amen, the faithful and true Witness, the Beginning of the creation of God.*

15 *I know thy works, that thou art neither cold nor hot : I would thou wert cold or hot.*

16 *So then because thou art lukewarm, and neither cold nor hot, I will spue thee out of my mouth.*

Laodicea was an opulent city upon the river Lycus, situated not far from Colossæ, as we learn from the association of these two churches in St. Paul's Epistle to the Colossians, ch. iv. There is a wonderful sublimity and comprehension in the titles which Christ assumes to himself in this address to the angel of the Laodicean church. The appellation " Amen " conveys to us, that as in Christ all the promises and prophecies centre, so is he pledged by the appropriation of this title to himself to the steadfast fulfilment of them :

it represents his stability, in opposition to the variableness of every other creature. This dignity seems to be peculiarly attached to the promise of Christ's advent, (see ch. i. 7. and xxii. 20.) as though to give this glorious truth a double surety in the eyes of men, because the Holy Ghost foresaw " that in the last days there should arise scoffers, who should say, Where is the promise of his coming?" (2 Pet. iii. 4.)

The expression also signifies the ratification or confirmation of a covenant. All the promises of old were given on condition of man's obedience, but none performed the requirements of God till Christ fulfilled the law, which having done, he gathered them all into himself, as his own indefeasible right, and thus became the great Amen to all that had been written in the law. He is " the faithful and true Witness ; " the same expression occurs in the inscription in chap. i. 5, and also when he comes in judgment on the infidel Antichrist and the false prophet. (chap. xix. 11:) As a witness, he is to be regarded as testifying of the Father, of whom none but the Son could be a true and faithful witness, because he alone had been with the Father from the beginning. This title

17 *Because thou sayest, I am rich, and increased with goods, and have need of nothing ; and knowest not that thou art wretched and miserable, and poor, and blind, and naked.*

18 *I counsel thee to buy of me gold tried in the fire that thou mayest be rich ; and white raiment, that thou mayest be clothed, and that the shame of thy nakedness do not appear ; and anoint thine eyes with eyesalve, that thou mayest see.*
19 *As many as I love, I rebuke and chasten ; be zealous therefore, and repent.*

20 *Behold, I stand at the door and knock ; if any man hear my voice, and open the door, I will come in to him, and will sup with him, and he with me.*

21 *To him that overcometh will I grant to sit with me in my throne, even as I also overcame, and am set down with my Father in his throne.*

22 *He that hath an ear let him hear what the Spirit saith unto the churches.*

carries with it conviction, not only of the pre-existence of our Saviour, but also of his distinct personality from the Father. To constitute a witness, it is requisite that he should have seen the person witnessed of (see John xv. 27 ; iii. 11 ; v. 36) ; and, accordingly we find it declared, that " the Word was with God in the beginning;" and " that no man hath seen God at any time, but the Son, which is in the bosom of the Father" (John i, 1, 2 and 18) : also, that the persons should be distinct, for no man can be a witness in his own cause. Distinction of persons, therefore, and knowledge of the party witnessed of, are essential to a true witness.

He is " the Beginning of the creation of God." The manifestation of the Godhead in the creature form was the first grand object of the creation ; and to which every other created thing was to be considered subordinate. He was the first in the purpose of God, though not in the manifestation. Adam, and all that went before, was but a type or foreshewing of him that was to come. It does not appear that our Lord brings any charge of false doctrine against the angel of the Laodicean church ; from which we may learn, that orthodoxy in doctrine does not necessarily ensure purity and holiness of life. An assent to established truths in religion, does not constitute a Christian, if the belief does not affect the heart, and influence the conduct ; for it is the life that evinces the true disciple. It is to be feared that there are two many in this flowery day of profession, who talk of brotherly love, and other Christian graces, but who find it very inconvenient and troublesome to be required to exhibit it in action. The Laodicean church was exposed to the temptation of prosperity, both in spiritual and temporal affairs ; and she fell into the snare from which few escape, who are similarly tried ; she became lukewarm and indifferent. If men were really conscious of the evil influence of riches, surely they would not be so eager in acquiring the glittering snare. Many can endure adversity who fall at the first onset of a course of prosperity ; for, though the force of the expression seems to be now explained away, yet it is equally true, as when our Saviour uttered it, " How hardly shall a rich man enter into the kingdom of heaven !"

He that overcometh is promised to sit with Christ in his throne even as he also overcame, and is sat down in his father's throne. Here is a manifest distinction observed between the Father's throne and Christ's throne : the saints are promised a participation in the latter, but they never shall expect to obtain the former.

It is the same promise as that conveyed to the church at Thyatira; a share in the glory and dominion of Christ's reign, over the universe, as it is written in one sublime and comprehensive expression in this book (Rev. xxi. 7), "He that overcometh shall inherit all things."

Laodicea, after the many fluctuations of the Greek Empire in Asia, sunk in the general decay, and is now a heap of ruins. There is a small village called Eskihisar near its site, containing about fifty inhabitants, and two solitary Christians*, who are the only melancholy remnant, to record that a church once existed at Laodicea.

---

* Lindsay's Letters.

CHAPTER IV.

Christ revealed as Prince of the kings of the earth, in the fourth and fifth Chapters, being prefatory to the sixth, which properly commences the prophecies of the sealed book.

CHRIST having revealed himself in the character of universal Bishop, in the foregoing Epistles to the seven churches, we find in the following chapters, he is introduced in the Apostle's vision, as the King-Priest; and prevailing to open that sealed book, which none other, save him, in heaven or earth, could accomplish. The prophetic parts of this book are composed of detached chronological histories, each of which is separately introduced by an appropriate preface. As the prophecies which extend through this Revelation, from the sixth chapter, contain events, included in all time, until the second advent of our Lord, the whole is ushered into notice, with a peculiar dignity and circumstance, corresponding to the magnitude and sublimity of the Revelation. We consider, therefore, the two following chapters as introductory to that which follows.

In the first verse, our Lord himself informs the Apostle that he is now entering on the things which should be hereafter (chap. i. 19); and the seer is conscious of a sudden transition from contemplating the state of the Asiatic churches, to a vision in heaven. A door was opened in heaven; that is, into the secret and invisible; not a place, except so far as the body of Christ, wherever it is, gives it that name; as a place it is only contemplated in the Divine counsel. It describes the invisible as distinguished from the visible; it is the condition of existence of angels, separate spirits, and invisible beings. The Apos-

1 *After this I looked, and, behold, a door was opened in heaven; and the first voice which I heard was as it were of a trumpet talking with me; which said, Come up hither, and I will shew thee things which must be hereafter.*

tle heard a voice, as it were of a trumpet speaking to him (chap. i. 10.) This similitude is used to denote the voice of Christ, or of the church in heaven; and as we learn from chap. xix. 10, and xxii. 9, that this vision was communicated through one who confessed himself to be of St. John's fellow servants, the prophets, we conclude that in this case it represented the latter.

2 *And immediately I was in the Spirit; and, behold, a throne was set in heaven, and one sat on the throne.*

3 *And he that sat was to look upon like a jasper and a sardine stone: and there was a rainbow round about the throne, in sight like unto an emerald.*

The Apostle is here presented with a sublime representation of Christ, seated on a throne, as King. He was to look upon, like a jasper and a sardine stone; from the addition to the former, in chap. xxi. 11, having a similitude to jasper, and clear as crystal, it does not appear to be the stone usually described as a jasper, but the diamond.—In the above passage, the jasper stone is emblematical of the glory of God; the sardine stone is of a blood-red or flesh colour: a combination of these two symbols conveys to us the glory of the Godhead, seen through the human nature of Christ. A rainbow surrounded the throne, in sight like unto an emerald— that is, of a green hue, the colour most grateful to the eye. The rainbow is God's token of the covenant made with Noah (Gen. ix. 17); and as the throne seen by the Apostle was approachable only through the rainbow, so we cannot draw nigh unto God save through that covenant of mercy made with our Mediator Jesus Christ. The rainbow is formed by the rays of the sun lighting upon the descending particles of water, and by them refracted: so the "rainbow surrounding the throne" may be considered as formed by the beams of that Sun of Righteousness, who is the only source of spiritual life, thrown upon the promises contained in the covenant, which only thus receives its glory, or is capable of being apprehended by the believer's faith.

The vision presents Christ to us as our great Covenant Head, in his priestly character; and likewise God the Father seen in Christ on the throne, the person of the Father exhibited or presented in Christ; the great mystery of the Trinity consisting in the essential invisibility of the Father, and that the object of worship should ever continue unseen. A similar vision occurs in Dan. vii. 9, also Ezek. i.

The four and twenty elders compose a circle round the throne, in the form of the Jewish Sanhedrim. The expression here, is to receive explanation by the consideration of the character, as comprehended in the Jewish, and not in the Christian economy; and upon reference to the Pentateuch, it will be found rather to convey the idea of a governor or judge, than as pertaining to Christian church-discipline. Their having crowns of gold on their heads, and being clothed with white raiment, point out their character as priests and kings. The white garments were worn by the high priest, when he went into the holy of holies, and is here expressive of the church within the vail; that is, in the heavens. The elders represent the church as having received this kingdom (see chap. v, 8—10) which passage is conclusive as to the correctness of this interpretation.

> *4 And round about the throne were four and twenty seats: and upon the seats I saw four and twenty elders sitting, clothed in white raiment; and they had on their heads crowns of gold.*

These characteristics of judgment, proceeding from the throne, (see also chap. viii. 5; xi. 19; xvi. 18,) exhibit to us a truth too much forgotten, that though Christ will keep his covenant with those who lay hold of it by faith, yet that there remains an awful day of reckoning, for those who have trampled upon and despised it, and counted it an unholy thing. The latter clause of the verse, as has been previously explained (see note to chap. i. 4), sets forth the Holy Ghost in diffusion, but still maintaining his oneness of character. Seven is a perfect or complete number, representing diffusion gathered into union. The science of music illustrates this truth: sound being determined by seven distinct notes, an eighth would resolve itself into the first again, and thus describe a circle—the emblem of completeness and of perpetuity. The same truth is also illustrated from the nature and properties of colours. There are seven principal colours; an eighth therefore can only be a varia-

> *5 And out of the throne proceeded lightnings and thunderings and voices: and there were seven lamps of fire burning before the throne, which are the seven Spirits of God.*

tion of one of the seven, or a mixture of some portions of them.

6 *And before the throne there was a sea of glass like unto crystal: and in the midst of the throne, and round about the throne, were four beasts full of eyes before and behind.*

7 And the first beast was like a lion, and the second beast like a calf, and the third beast had a face as a man, and the fourth beast was like a flying eagle.

The sea of glass, like unto crystal, signifies the state of unruffled calmness and peacefulness of all before the throne. The word translated beasts, is better rendered living creatures; as in Ezek. i. 5, and in chap. x., which evidently contain a similar vision, and wherein the same appearances are denominated cherubims. We have seen the church in its kingly character, represented in this chapter, verse 4, under the emblem of twenty-four elders. The living creatures reveal her in her wilderness, or militant condition marching round the ark, and supporting Christ's kingly power. The emblem appears to be taken from the order in which the twelve tribes of Israel were arranged in their march through the wilderness. (Num. ii.) The tabernacle being placed in the centre, the tribes were thus disposed of: Judah to the east, with two tribes, under his standard of a lion; Reuben to the south, with two tribes, under his standard of the face of a man; Ephraim, on the west side, with two tribes, under his standard of a young bull; and Dan, to the north, with two tribes, under his standard of an eagle. The powerful and dominant character of the symbols chosen, leave no alternative than the conclusion that they denote that church which shall yet be made kings and priests unto God, and be thereby installed into supremacy over all creation. They are not in possession of the power—as the crowned elders—but progressing in its acquirement. It is for these reasons that the four living creatures are supposed to denote the church on earth. But that they have some representative character of the church is put beyond all doubt, by a reference to the following chapter, v. 8 —10; wherein they are uniting with the elders in ascriptions of praise and glory to him who was slain, and had redeemed them to God by his blood, out of every kindred, and tongue, and people, and nation, and are looking forward to reigning on the earth, which promise exclusively belongs to the saints of God.

The church militant is here presented to us, as not resting day or night, but as continually ascribing Holiness to the Lord God Almighty, with thanksgivings. This characterises the constant watchfulness necessary to such a state of warfare; and their being full of eyes, appears to convey the truth, that the church on earth are the grand manifestators of God's providence. It is God the Father, seen in Christ that is the object of worship on the throne, and who is designated by that title, only applicable to the eternal Godhead, having neither beginning nor end. (see chap. i.)

The homage which the four and twenty elders pay to Him that sat on the throne is that due unto the King of kings as their supreme Head; and Christ as the representative and manifestation of the person of the Father, receives the worship of all created things both in heaven and on the earth.

8 *And the four beasts had each of them six wings about him; and they were full of eyes within: and they rest not day and night, saying, Holy, holy, holy, Lord God Almighty, which was, and is, and is to come.*

9 *And when those beasts give glory and honour and thanks to him that sat on the throne, who liveth for ever and ever.*

10 *The four and twenty elders fall down before him that sat on the throne, and worship him that liveth for ever and ever, and cast their crowns before the throne, saying,*

11 *Thou art worthy, O Lord, to receive glory and honour and power; for thou hast created all things, and for thy pleasure they are and were created.*

The elders casting their crowns before the throne, and their ascription of all power to him, by whom and for whom all things were made, is the acknowledgment to their great King; that it is from him they receive, and for his pleasure they employ their delegated honours. This act of homage receives illustration from the coronation of a Christian prince, whose nobles surround the throne, remaining uncovered with their coronets in their hands until the king is crowned; when they place them on their heads, to signify, that it is from him, as their earthly sovereign, all their possessions and honours are derived.

CHAPTER V.

1 *And I saw in the right hand of him that sat on the throne a book written within and on the backside, sealed with seven seals.*

2 *And I saw a strong angel proclaiming with a loud voice, Who is worthy to open the book, and to loose the seals thereof?*

3 *And no man in heaven, nor in earth, neither under the earth, was able to open the book, neither to look thereon.*

4 *And I wept much, because no man was found worthy to open and to read the book, neither to look thereon.*

THIS book, seen in the right hand of him that sat upon the throne, was rather a roll, sealed with seven seals, written within and without: that is, its contents were full and complete, each seal containing a separate mystery, which it would be necessary to break to arrive at. This sealed book formed a part of this Apocalypse, in which is included all the events of God's providence, and the demonstration of his power, until the consummation of all things.

The highest importance and dignity is attached to this book in heaven; and notwithstanding the proclamation of the angel, no one is found able to open it, neither to look thereon. The Apostle, wrapt in the spirit, is overwhelmed with disappointment, having been seized with an earnest desire to become acquainted with its contents: and he wept much, because no one was found worthy to open and to read it. By which we may learn that it is not the mark of an unholy and culpable curiosity, to search into the purposes of God, as revealed in his word. (See also chap. i. 1, 3, xiii, 18, and xxii. 18, 19.)

5 *And one of the elders saith unto me, Weep not: behold the Lion of the tribe of Juda, the Root of David, hath prevailed to open the book, and to loose the seven seals thereof.*

The anxiety which the Apostle evinced to become acquainted with the mysteries of this book, evidently meets with the Divine approbation; for one of the elders is sent to inform him that there is one who can accomplish the arduous task—even the

Lion of the tribe of Judah. This affords us another proof, that this sealed book is included in the Apocalypse; which, we are informed in chap. i. 1, "God gave unto Jesus Christ to shew unto his servants things which must shortly come to pass." The appellations given unto Christ here pertain to his manhood— and shew us that it is to Him, as Son of Man, this revelation is given.

Christ having been represented as the great King, he is here introduced as the atoning sacrifice, the Lamb slain from before the foundations of the world. The great High Priest, who, by the one sacrifice of himself, hath for ever put away sin.

It is in this chapter that he prevails to open the book (see v. 9); for it was that in which he suffered, being made perfect through suffering. The act of God's giving this revelation to him spoken of, chap. i. 1, is here narrated.

6 *And I beheld, and, lo, in the midst of the throne and of the four beasts, and in the midst of the elders, stood a Lamb as it had been slain, having seven horns and seven eyes, which are the seven Spirits of God sent forth into all the earth.*

7 *And he came and took the book out of the right hand of him that sat upon the throne.*

The Lamb had seven horns and seven eyes. The horn is emblematical of power (Deut. xxxiii. 17), and conveys to us the idea of that given unto Christ after his resurrection, when he said. "All power is given unto me in heaven and in earth." (Matt. xxviii. 18.) The seven eyes are interpreted in the text to be the seven Spirits of God—and are here introduced, particularly as indicative of Christ's omniscience and discernment. We have before observed, that the sevenfold representation of the Spirit of God instructs us in the mystery of the Holy Ghost, diffused over, and possessed by, an extended yet a limited and complete number. And we learn also from this text, that great truth, supported by all Scripture, that Jesus Christ is endued in his priesthood by the Father with the gift of the Holy Ghost; and that it is he that sends him forth into all the earth—unto as many as God the Father shall see fit in the good pleasure of his will to give unto him. As it is a most important point of sound doctrine, that the person of the Father is only seen in Jesus Christ, it was necessary—as Christ had to represent two distinct characters in this vision, namely, that of the Father on the throne, and his own as Priest—that the machinery of the prophecy should be so arranged, as to present the appearance of two persons, though, in fact, it is only Christ that is seen throughout. A similar vision takes place in Daniel, chap. vii. 22.

8 *And when he had taken the book, the four beasts and four and twenty elders fell down before the Lamb, having every one of them harps and golden vials full of odours, which are the prayers of saints.*

9 *And they sang a new song, saying, Thou art worthy to take the book, and to open the seals thereof: for thou wast slain, and hast redeemed us to God by thy blood out of every kindred, and tongue, and people, and nation;*

10 *And hast made us unto our God kings and priests: and we shall reign on the earth.*

In the previous chapter the elders take the precedency in their higher function of kings; but here the four living creatures are first mentioned, because it is in his character as Lamb that Christ obtains the book, therefore the living creatures are first to celebrate the act. They had harps and vials full of odours. There had been no event in heaven to call forth such loud hosannahs, as the redemption of a fallen creation by the blood of the Lamb; and therefore they tuned their harps to sing a new song of praise and of prayer.

This passage affords us conclusive evidence that the twenty-four elders and four living creatures will admit of no other interpretation than the church in heaven—for those only could sing this new song who had been redeemed out of every kindred and tongue, and people and nation. This interesting representation of the church in heaven, before the resurrection, likewise establishes the conscious blessedness of redeemed souls after death and their active employment in the service of their Lord. It conveys to us, likewise, the important intelligence, that they are still in a longing condition, waiting for the consummation of their happiness—when they shall be endued with power and holiness, made kings and priests, and reign with Christ on the earth. They are the same characters under the fifth seal, chap. vi. 10, who are crying out to God to avenge their blood on them that dwell on the earth, for they knew that the day of his vengeance was the year of their full recompense. (Is. xxxiv. 8.) Accordingly we find, after Christ's coming, set forth in the nineteenth chapter, when he destroys, at the battle of Armageddon, the beast of infidelity and the false prophet of Rome, with the armies of the kings of the earth; that the twentieth chapter introduces us into this millennial reign of the saints, which all enjoy who have been made participators in the first resurrection.

The angels are here represented encompassing as a guard the elders and living creatures, and looking upon the mystery of an elect Church standing ready to fulfil their office of ministering spirits (Heb. i. 14,) to the church of Christ.

The church in heaven (see v. 9, 10) sing of redemption and of electing love, and conclude with the delightful anticipation of being made kings and priests unto God; but the angels celebrate his power over creation, and ascribe the possession and dominion of all things to him who is creation's Lord. They waited for the song of the church, and then added their hosannahs of praise and sevenfold ascription of power and glory to the Lamb that was slain, yet liveth for ever and ever.

Here the whole visible creation join in this song of praise; all creatures both in heaven and earth ascribe to Him that sitteth upon the throne blessing, and honour, and glory, (see Ps. cxlviii. and Rom. viii. 19, 22.)

They now contemplate the two persons in one substance, two seen in one; the Father ruling for Christ until he hath put all things under his feet (Ps. cx. 1), and Christ ac-

11 *And I beheld, and I heard the voice of many angels round about the throne and the beasts and the elders: and the number of them was ten thousand times ten thousand, and thousands of thousands;*

12 *Saying with a loud voice, Worthy is the Lamb that was slain to receive power, and riches, and wisdom, and strength, and honour, and glory, and blessing.*

13 *And every creature which is in heaven, and on the earth, and under the earth, and such as are in the sea, and all that are in them, heard I saying, Blessing, and honour, and glory, and power, be unto him that sitteth upon the throne and unto the Lamb for ever and ever.*

14 *And the four beasts*

said, Amen. And the four and twenty elders fell down and worshipped him that liveth for ever and ever. knowledged as the manifested head of all power in heaven and earth.

This sublime and comprehensive vision is concluded as it begun, (chap. iv.) by a simultaneous act of worship from the church, addressed to Him that sitteth on the throne, and that liveth for ever and ever.

CHAPTER VI.

The prophecies of the sealed book commence with this chapter.

The contents of the book seen in the right hand of him that sat on the throne, and which only the Lion of the tribe of Judah prevailed to open, (chap. v.) are in this, and the following chapters, revealed to the Apostle. They represent seven successive acts of power, by which the enemies of Christ's church are scattered, and thereby the way prepared for the establishment of his own kingdom. The seven seals respect the western branch of the Roman empire—the fourth monarchy, or ten kingdoms of Daniel (chap. ii. 44, and vii. 23, 27). In the first four

1 *And I saw when the Lamb opened one of the seals, and I heard, as it were the noise of thunder, one of the four beasts* (representing the church in her prophetical and priestly character, chap. iv. 6, v. 8) *saying, Come and see.*

2 *And I saw, and behold a white horse: and he that sat on him* (Constantine) *had a bow; and a crown was given unto him: and he went forth conquering, and to conquer.*

seals, we have four successive emperors; in whose times, and by whose chief instrumentality, Paganism, the first enemy of the church, was judged and brought to its end. In chap. ii. 10, we find a reference to ten years' persecution which the church at Smyrna was to undergo, and which we have referred to that period of Diocletian's reign, when the Christians underwent that sore trial. As this was included in that portion of this book, denominated " the things which are," according to Christ's own division of the prophecy (chap. i. 19), it is evident we must not look for this commencing act of retribution on Paganism until after this period, A. D. 303—312. During the first three centuries of the Christian era, the church experienced from the Pagan Roman emperors one continued course of persecutions; interrupted during that whole period only by occasional variations in severity and barbarity. After the death of Diocletian, Constantine the Great was raised to the throne of the Roman Empire, A. D. 306. He is represented as seated on a white horse, emblematical of imperial power and of conquest. He gave the first blow to Paganism by constituting Christianity the established religion of the empire, which took place after his conversion, A. D. 312. It is related of him, that in a vision he saw a cross, with this inscription, "In this overcome;" and Eusebius records, that such ever after continued to be his motto. "Constantine gave the most perfect toleration to Christians through the whole extent of his dominions; Providence was still with him in enlarging his kingdom, that, like another Cyrus, he might give peace and liberty to the church*."

3 And when he had opened the second seal, I heard the second beast say, Come and see.

4 And there went out another horse that was red: (emblematical of war and bloodshed) *and power was given to him* (Theodosius) *that sat thereon to take peace from the earth,* (by civil war,) *and that they should kill one another: and there was given* unto *him a great sword.*

During the reign of Constantine the Great, after his conversion, A. D. 312, and for many successive years, Christianity enjoyed comparative protection; but in the year 361, Julian the Apostate, Constantine's nephew, succeeded Constantius, and openly declared for Paganism†. Julian reigned one year and eight months, during which period he exerted the most consummate artifice and the most unwearied perseverance, to exterminate Christianity and to re-establish Paganism. These objects he proposed effecting more by a systematic course of artful policy, than by the exercise of open violence; and truly, for the short period of his reign, Paganism owned a most active apostle. Amongst the extraordinary expedients to which he resorted, to vilify and degrade the Christian religion, one deserves particular notice, from its singular conception and its audacious impiety. Perceiving the dispersion of the Jews, and the continued desolation of their Temple to be predicted of in the prophecies, he encouraged the

* See Milner's Church History, vol. ii. p 31.
† See a full account of Julian's introduction of Paganism, in Milner's Church History, vol. ii. chap. x, who has himself followed Cave's History of the Julian Apostacy, in his History of the Fathers, sect. iii. p. 284.

D

Jews to rebuild it; his design being to oppose the truth of the prophetic record, and thus to prove Christ's prediction an imposture. For this purpose he committed the execution of the affair to Alypius of Antioch, who was assisted by the governor of the province; but an earthquake, attended with horrible balls of fire breaking out near the foundations, rendered the place inaccessible to the terrified workmen, and the enterprise was ultimately relinquished. Marvellous as this story may appear, it has the authority of ecclesiastical writers of unquestioned credibility, many of whom lived at the period; amongst these are Gregory Nazianzen, Ambrose, and Chrysosotm, with many others, as well as of the Jewish rabbis*. But it was vain for him to contend with Omnipotence. He received a mortal wound in his expedition against the Persians. It is recorded of him, that, conscious of his approaching end, he exclaimed, " O, Galilean! Thou hast conquered" After Julian's death, a succession of emperors came to the throne, variously disposed towards Christianity and Paganism; but the periods of their reign were too short to enable any one to effect a permanent alteration in favour of either, until Theodosius the Great (v. 4.) became master of the Roman Empire, originally raised from a private condition to the imperial dignity by the emperor Gratian.

Paganism sought again to rally itself under the usurpers **Maximus** and **Eugenius**; the former governing in Britain, A. D. 383—the latter, who usurped the empire of the West, by the murder of the emperor Valentinius. But Theodosius who reigned in the East, after a civil war in which he took peace from the earth (v. 4), defeated and killed the former, A. D 388† : and the latter met a similar fate soon after his usurpation‡. Theodosius having thus become sole governor of the Roman Empire, set himself to the extirpation of the Pagan idolatry with the most decisive vigour. He destroyed all the Pagan temples and made it a capital crime to sacrifice or attend the Pagan rites‖. Paganism never lifted up its head in strength after this;

* Warburton's Julian—also Cave's Lives of the Fathers—S. Cyril of Jerusalem, p. 561.
† Eusebius Ecclesiast. Hist. lib. **v.** chap. **xiv.** p. 333.
‡ Eusebius Ecclesiast. Hist. lib. v. chap. xxv. p. 350.
‖ Cave's Introduction to the Lives of the Fathers, vol. ii. **sect. 5.**

and though it still lingered on an existence until the fourth seal, habit alone supported it, and the fourth century closes with the establishment of Christianity in the Róman empire as the religion of the state*.

5 *And when he had opened the third seal, I heard the third beast say, Come and see. And I beheld, and lo a black horse,* (emblematical of defeat, the reverse of white,) *and he that sat on him* (Honorius) *had a pair of balances in his hand.*

6 *And I heard a voice in the midst of the four beasts say, A measure of wheat for a penny, and three measures of barley for a penny; and see thou hurt not the oil and wine.*

Though Paganism, as a system, was by these two blows of the first and second seals, wounded to death throughout the empire, yet it still lived in Rome; from which, as from a centre of Satan's tyrannic power, had issued all those successive persecutions which had assailed the Christian church since her establishment, filling the whole empire with the blood of her martyrs. Accordingly we find the judgments of the third seal directed towards Pagan Rome and her dependencies. God visits a nation for her national crimes, committed as a collective body—whose guilt he allows to accumulate from generation to generation, until her iniquity is full and she has thus ripened herself for the Divine vengeance.

The opening of the third seal presents us with the emblems of an emperor; but neither with the bow of far-ranging conquest, nor with the great sword of civil warfare, but with a pair of balances in his hand; signifying that his power should be taken up not with arms, but with weighing and measuring, in exact scales, the allowances of his people; in what kind is taught us by the interpretation of a voice, saying, "A measure of wheat for a penny, and three measures of barley for a penny, (prices for the necessaries of life, indicative of famine;) and see thou hurt not the oil and the wine;" which expression points out the unusual care to be observed of these articles of life. He rode upon a black horse, indicating the reverse of conquest; namely, defeat, sorrow, and dejection. This heavy affliction fell upon the city of Rome, in the time of the emperor Honorius; when

---

* Milner's Church History, vol. ii, p. 207.

Alaric the Goth, after three devastations of Italy, and two beleaguerments of the capital, at length took and sacked it, A. D. 410, sparing the Christians, and putting another hand to the Pagan superstition in the conflagration of the Heathen temples*. Italy remained in possession of the Goths till A. D. 414, when it was evacuated by treaty.

The fourth seal contains a second judgment upon the Roman empire, which came to pass in the reign of Justinian, falling particularly on Africa and Italy (the fourth part of the Roman earth). The rider on the pale or livid horse—indicative of corruption—represents the emperor Justinian: and he is called death, or the Destroyer; to denote the enormous destruction of human life, that should attend the flux and reflux of conquest, of which that portion of the Roman empire was made the theatre. Italy was so laid waste by this devastating war, carried on by his general Belisarius, who took Rome from the Goths, A. D. 536, and ultimately expelled them from Italy, that many of her fairest provinces relapsed into a state of savage nature, and the country became so depopulated, that wild beasts began to gain the ascendancy over man (v. 8.) Famine and disease, the usual accompaniments of the sword, came in this terrific train of desolating judgment ; and thus the four scourges of the human race mentioned in the text, slaughter, famine, pestilence, and wild beasts, had during this period exerted by turns their exterminating ravages over the whole of Italy. Thus have we in four great acts of God, working through the instrumentality of human power, the process by which he overthrew Paganism, the first great enemy of the church of Christ. This interpretation receives

7 *And when he had opened the fourth seal,* **I heard the voice** of the **fourth beast say, Come and see.**
8 *And I looked, and behold* **a pale horse:** (of a livid green, the colour of corruption:)*and his name that sat on him was* Death, and Hell followed with him (Justinian). *And power was* given unto them over the *fourth part of earth,* (that is, one of the four prefectures into which the Roman empire was divided by Constantine) *to kill* with sword, and with hunger, *and with death, and* **with the beasts of the earth.**

* Irving's Babylon Foredoomed, vol. i. p. 185.

remarkable confirmation, from the fact that Echard, and most historians, when treating of that period of the Roman history in which we have traced the fulfilment of the first four seals, from A. D. 312 to A. D. 536, narrates the historical events in these four grand divisions. History is but a comment on prophecy. Indeed it has not an object, if not applied to develop the purposes of God, and display the manifestations of his providence amongst the nations of the earth.

9 *And when he had opened the fifth seal, I saw under the altar the souls of them that were slain for the word of God, and for the testimony which they held:* (during the period of the Pagan persecutions)

10 *And they cried with a loud voice, saying, How long, O Lord, holy and true, dost thou not judge and avenge our blood on them that dwell on the earth?*

11 *And white robes were given unto every one of them ; and it was said unto them, that they should rest yet for a little season,* (that is, the period of 1260 years during which the saints were given into the hands of the little horn of Daniel, which is the Papacy : see Dan. vii. 25,) *until their fellow-servants also and their brethren, that should be killed* (by the Papal persecutions) *as they were* (by the Pagan), *should be fulfilled.*

Paganism having thus been suppressed and rooted up, so that scarcely any vestige of it remained ; we find the fifth seal introduces to us another form of superstition, which was designed in the Divine purpose, to have the ascendency over the saints of God, for its limited period.

At the opening of the fifth seal, the Apostle sees a vision in heaven. The altar stood in the temple : and when the victim was sacrificed, the blood was received below—the blood is the life. The souls under the altar, therefore represent the martyrs who had been slain by the Pagan persecution. This heavenly vision is not to be considered in time, subsequent to the previous seals, but as a cry for vengeance, on their persecutors, which had continued through, and of which, those judgments wer[e] the consequence. White robes were put on by the priests, when they entered into the holiest of all ; and this figure here represents (verse 9) the saints who had been martyred, as having entered into heaven itself. When the Pagan judgments had terminated, they were expecting that their enemies should be judged, and that they should realize the fulfilment of that promise, to which they were looking (under another symbol, in chap. v. 10) with so much desire, to reign on the earth with Christ, but they are told they must wait a little season (chap. xii. 12), until their brethren should be likewise killed (ver. 11) by another form of superstition, the Papacy, and accordingly they are found rejoicing, when her judgment takes place, (see chap. **xvi. 5**, and xix. 2.) This fifth seal therefore takes in the whole compass of that **Papal** period; but gives no particulars of its fulfilment, because it is not comprehended in the purpose of prophecy to give the growth of evil powers, but to shew forth their punishment **when** arrived at maturity; and also, because they are given during this period of forty-two months, or 1260 days in the **xith** chapter.

It is admitted by all Protestant commentators, with scarcely one exception, that the time, times, and the dividing of time of Daniel, during which the saints were to be given into the power of the little horn, is the period of 1260 years of the Papacy (a time, according to the Jewish computation, being 360 years; times, being double, and the dividing of time half that period). There can be little doubt that if we can ascertain the completion of the Pagan persecution, we shall have made **great** progress in fixing the rise of the Papal: for it is to be supposed, that Satan no sooner found himself defeated in one form of enmity to the church, than he would instantly assume another; otherwise if an interval were admitted to occur between the extinction of the one, and the rise of the other, the church would, during such time, be exempt from Satan's malice: which is altogether inconsistent with the activity that he has ever manifested against the truth. If therefore, as we think we have satisfactorily shewn, in our interpretation of the fourth seal, that Paganism, after enduring repeated shocks from the Arian nations, which for this purpose God brought upon the Roman Empire, **was** finally put down and extinguished in the reign of Justinian; and to no other period in history can its extinction be traced; it is likewise in this reign we must expect to find a commencing date to this new persecuting power, referred to in this seal, and which, we learn from Daniel, is to last 1260 years (Dan. vii, 25, 26), at the expiration of which the judgment is to sit, and his dominion is to be taken away.

There has arisen no question in the prophetic writings more important, or one which has occasioned deservedly more discussion than that of fixing the commencement of this Papal period of 1260 years; because, if ascertained, an addition of seventy-five years, at its termination, would lead us to that time which Daniel pronounced to be blessed ; and as he is promised to stand in his lot, it can mean none other than the first resurrection, and the coming of our Lord. It is only within the last few years, that any unanimity has existed upon this interesting subject ; and we can venture to affirm, that little diversity of opinion is now entertained by modern commentators, and the students of prophecy. The question is, at what time were the saints given into the hands of the Papacy ; and we shall find the answer remarkably to coincide with our supposition, that it must be found in the reign of Justinian, when Paganism was finally put down, and never afterwards raised its head as a persecuting power. By an edict, bearing date March, 533, authority was given to the Bishop of Rome to settle all controversies in the church, of which he was declared to be the infallible head, *and power was given him by such enacted law of the empire, against whomsoever he deemed heretical.* It was not merely one edict, but a systematic course of policy, whereby the Papacy was stamped the imperial religion ; (just as much as Christianity was by Constantine :) so that its very image is delineated in the beginning of Justinian's code of laws ; the celibacy of the clergy, the intercession of the Virgin Mary, the adoration of the cross, &c. &c. In fixing the year 533, as the commencement of the 1260 years, we have a corroborative proof, almost equal to demonstration, if the events spoken of in prophecy to take place at its termination should be found to receive an exact and minute accomplishment at the precise time. The expiration of the 1260 years therefore would occur, A. D. 1792 : and accordingly we find the events predicted in the sixth seal, which ended in the French Revolution of Aug. 10, 1792, accompanied with such a variety of minute particulars, presents us with an adequate fulfilment, which nothing but the truth itself could furnish.

Adding seventy-five years to 1792 will bring us down to 1867, by which time, we have no doubt, the day of wrath will have passed over—Christ's enemies be destroyed—and that blessed period will have arrived, when the saints are to possess the kingdom for ever and ever. (See also chap. xii. 16.)

In strict accordance with the observation last advanced, we find the sixth seal announced by a great earthquake on a portion of the Papal kingdoms, which was God's first act of retributive justice on that apostacy. The period of this seal is from A.D. 1789, occupying the four last years of the Papal period of 1260 years. It describes a popular revolution of an established government, with the total eclipse of the kingly power : the subversion of all authority, and the degradation and banishment of the dignities of the land.

The fourth monarchy of Daniel, (see chap. vii. 24,) or Roman Empire, now become Papal (Rev. xvii. 12), was to be divided into ten kingdoms ; and it is to be expected, if this seal only operated partially, that such kingdom would be selected by God, that had most prominently distinguished herself in the erection and support of the Papal hierarchy. Accordingly, we find, on consulting history, that in the reign of Pepin of France, the most considerable accessions of territory and temporal power were secured to the Pope, chiefly through his instrumentality, A. D. 705 ; and that subsequently his son and successor, Charlemagne, sub-

12 *And I beheld when he had opened the sixth seal, and, lo, there was a great earthquake* (popular revolution) ; *and the sun became black as sackcloth of hair,* (eclipse of kingly power,) *and the moon became as blood,* (death of a queen).

13 *And the stars of heaven* (the nobles of the political hemisphere) *fell unto the earth* (degraded in dignity to the common level , *even as a fig-tree casteth her untimely figs when she is shaken of a mighty wind.*

14 *And the heaven* (political government) *departed as a scroll when it is rolled together ; and every mountain and island* (eminences of power and authority) *were moved out of their places.*

15 *And the kings of the earth, and the great men, and the rich men, and the chief captains, and the mighty* **men**, *and every bondman, and every free-*

man, hid themselves in the dens and in the rocks of the mountains.

16 And said to the mountains and rocks, Fall on us and hide us from the face of him that sitteth on the throne, and from the wrath of the Lamb:

17 For the great day of his wrath is come; and who shall be able to stand?

dued for him the kingdom of Lombardy, A.D. 774, and invested him with considerable portions of the conquered territory. France has likewise ever presented herself a willing instrument to persecute the true saints of God; for there is no nation whose historic records are so deeply stained with the blood of the martyrs of Christ. The persecutions of the Waldenses and Albigenses in the thirteenth century*, and, in later times, the massacres of her Protestant subjects, sufficiently mark her pre-eminence in the annals of blood, to direct our expectations to her, as the first object of Divine wrath. Accordingly, we find the prophecies contained in this seal receive a most remarkable accomplishment in France, to the very letter; and which, commencing in the year 1789, ran through four years of political contention, finally terminating in the memorable revolution of Aug. 10, 1792: when the king was deprived of all power, and ultimately ended his life upon a scaffold, Jan. 21, 1793. This is the same king prophesied of in Daniel xi. 20; the raiser of taxes, who was to precede the vile person, or the wilful king, Napoleon Bonaparte.

The stars of heaven are said to fall as untimely figs, and the islands to be only moved out of their places, because the time was not arrived for their final destruction; this being reserved for the last act of wrath, under the seventh vial, when it is said (chap. xvi. 20), "and every island fled away, and the mountains were not found." Accordingly, we find, that at, and subsequent to, that period, every dynasty in the ten Papal kingdoms of Europe, with the exception of England (see comment on chap. vii.), which had been established for centuries, were swept in the course of a few years from their eminence, carrying in their downfall all that adhered to them. They are now restored again—as at the first—we judge, preparatory to their demolition

---

* See Milner's Church History, vol. iii. chap. iv.

for ever. This seal derives additional importance from the consideration that the signs they contain are those by which the day of wrath and judgment is ushered in, every where throughout the prophecies, as preceding the glorious day of the coming of Christ, and his blessed reign upon the earth. And they stand here as a great mark of synchronism, with all that is written in the Prophets, from the time of Joel to the time of Christ.

The last three verses are anticipative, and prophetical of the great concluding act of God's wrath upon the Papal nations, of which this sixth seal was but a feeble type, introductory to the pouring out of the seven vials of wrath (see xvi. and three following chapters). A similar mark of synchronism in time is found in chap. ix. 20, after the sounding of the sixth trumpet, when the rest of the men are represented as not repenting. The final day of wrath is with more propriety referred to, in this instance, as taking effect on the western branch of the Roman empire, to which the seals have respect.

CHAPTER VII.

1 *And after these things I saw four angels standing on the four corners of the earth, holding the four winds of the earth, that the wind should not blow on the earth, nor on the sea, nor on any tree.*

2 *And I saw another angel ascending from the east having the seal of the living God: and he cried with a loud voice to the four angels, to whom it was given to hurt the earth and the sea.*

3 *Saying, Hurt not the earth, neither the sea, nor the trees, till we have sealed the servants of our God in their foreheads.*

4 *And I heard the number of them which were sealed: and there were sealed an hundred and forty and four thousand of all the tribes of the children of Israel.*

5 *Of the tribe of Juda were sealed twelve thousand. Of the tribe of Reuben were sealed twelve*

From the lamentations, in the latter part of the sixth seal, uttered by the kings and great men of the earth, who call upon the rocks to fall on them, because the great day of wrath was come, we should be led to conclude that the succeeding seal would contain the particulars of that day; but, on the contrary, the narrative being carried down to the sixth seal, and having sounded a note of coming judgment, we find this chapter commences by the sealing of a people, until the completion of which the four destroying angels are commanded not to hurt the earth. The structure of this book, as laid down in the Preface, would not allow of the opening of the seventh seal; but the Prophetic History of the Western branch of the Roman Empire having been brought down to that period, just preceding the last sevenfold act of consummating wrath (chap. xvi.), it was necessary to return, and bring the other two histories, down to the same point. The sealing, therefore, of the true servants of God is here introduced with perfect propriety; and the question arises, who are these favoured people? It is evidently a whole nation to whom this act of mercy is extended. The character of this book forbids our interpreting it literally; besides one of the tribes (Dan) is omitted, as if purposely, to prevent such an explanation; and also in the xiv th chapter, where the same sealed nation is spoken of, they are represented as following the Lamb whithersoever he goeth, which the Jews do not, but continue his greatest enemies. For these reasons, therefore, it cannot be the twelve tribes of Israel; and we are driven to the conclusion, that they are here introduced as a symbol to denote an entire nation, who should receive protection from the judgments contained under the seventh seal (chapter xvi.), in consequence of their being distinguished as a true church from the surrounding apostacy. Viewing this prophecy, therefore, as affecting the Western Roman earth, it may be asked,

thousand. Of the tribe of Gad were sealed twelve thousand.

6 Of the tribe of Aser were sealed twelve thousand. Of the tribe of Nephthalim were sealed twelve thousand. Of the tribe of Manasses were sealed twelve thousand.

7. Of the tribe of Simeon were sealed twelve thousand. Of the tribe of Levi were sealed twelve thousand. Of the tribe of Issachar were sealed twelve thousand.

8 Of the tribe of Zabulon were sealed twelve thousand. Of the tribe of Joseph were sealed twelve thousand. Of the tribe of Benjamin were sealed twelve thousand.

what nation answers to the description contained in the text? It is obvious the symbol can receive an adequate accomplishment only in the British Protestant nation. She alone, of all the ten Papal kingdoms, so effectually extricated herself from that apostacy at the time of the Reformation, as to present at this period a national church, founded upon the pure doctrines of the Bible; and she alone, of all these kingdoms, presents herself as receiving fulfilment of the prophecy by the most extraordinary exemption from the judgments which have been poured out since the year 1792, in the first six vials of wrath (chap xvi.), upon the other nine kingdoms of Christendom. Every capital in Christian Papal Europe, excepting England, has, in its turn, been possessed by the infidel Emperor of France, the country deluged with blood and rapine, and every dynasty and form of government therein brought down or disgraced, and trampled upon, by this scourge of the Papal nations. France, Spain, Austria, Portugal, Naples, Tuscany, and the three church-states in Italy, Lombardy, Ravenna, and Rome, have all in their turn experienced the heavy hand of this instrument of God's wrath; who has gone forth as a burning meteor, withering men by his presence, as though conscious of the Divine commission given him under the fourth vial, in the imperial symbol of the sun, to scorch men with fire. (chap. xvi. v. 8.)

9 *After this I beheld, and, lo, a great multitude, which no man could number, of all nations, and kindreds, and people, and tongues, stood before the throne, and before the Lamb clothed with white robes, and palms in their hands;*

10 *And cried with a loud voice, saying, Salvation to our God which sitteth upon the throne, and unto the Lamb.*

11 *And all the angels stood round about the throne, and about the elders and the four beasts, and fell before the throne on their faces, and worshipped God.*

12 *Saying, Amen: Blessing, and glory, and wisdom, and thanksgiving, and honour, and power, and might, be unto our God for ever and ever. Amen.*

13 *And one of the elders answered, saying unto me,*

It is evident that the vision which ensues in this chapter carries us on to a period subsequent to that event, predicted in the former part, from its introductory intimation that it was after this the Apostle beheld the great multitude which no man could number, of *all nations* and kindred, and people, and tongues, who stood before the throne: whereas the former vision consisted of a *single nation* whose express number is heard by the Apostle, and is therefore to be regarded as indicative of limitation. The symbols in the whole of this book are taken from the Jewish temple and service; and from the mention of the multitude before the throne having palms in their hands, we are referred to the feast of tabernacles, one of the three great feasts of the Jewish nation, when all Israel were present. See Lev. xxiii. 33—44.

The nation sealed in the former part of the chapter, are protected *during the pouring out of those judgments upon the rest of the nations:* but the vision here contemplates that peaceful condition of the church, when she shall be in the possession of the heavenly things, and which is subsequent to those acts of Divine wrath. It is contemporaneous with the feast of tabernacles predicted in Zechariah xiv. 16—19, which all the nations upon earth shall come up to Jerusalem to keep from year to year ; whilst the risen saints of God, shall serve him night and day, in that New Jerusalem which cometh down from heaven, chap. xxi. 2, xxii. 3.—5.— The above conclusion receives additional confirmation from the following considerations. In the 15th verse this glorious assemblage, who have been redeemed from much tribulation, are represented as being in the immediate presence of God, as having entered into the Holiest of all, in which interior recess of the temple, the throne of God was situated, and his glory appeared to the high priest, the antitype to which is unquestionably the Heavenly City. (chap. xxi. 22, to the end of the book) It is only when the seventh angel is to sound, when the kingdoms of this world become the kingdoms of our

What are these which are arrayed in white robes? and whence came they?

14 *And I said unto him, Sir, thou knowest. And he said to me, These are they which came out of great tribulation, and have washed their robes, and made them white in the blood of the Lamb.*

15 *Therefore are they before the throne of God, and serve him day and night in his temple ; and he that sitteth on the throne shall dwell among them.*

16 *They shall hunger no more, neither thirst any more ; neither shall the sun light on them, nor any heat.*

17 *For the Lamb which is in the midst of the throne shall feed them, and shall lead them unto living fountains of waters : and God shall wipe away all tears from their eyes.*

Lord and his Christ (chap. xi. 19), that the temple is said to be opened ; and in the xvth chapter we further learn, that though the temple is then opened, yet no man was able to enter into it, because it was filled with smoke of the glory of God and from his power, *until the seven plagues of the seven angels were fulfilled.* Now, as the last of the seven plagues contain the consummating act of the judgments in the battle of Armageddon, the destruction of the infidel Antichrist, and of the mystical Babylon, and which is immediately succeeded by Christ's millennial reign upon the earth, (see chap xvi. to xx.) it follows, as a necessary consequence, that the vision of the palm-bearing multitude, now under consideration, must represent the church in that state of blessedness during the Millennium, to which all the prophecies of this book, as well as every other, converges, as to a common centre. We are supported, in this conclusion, by a careful comparison of their condition, as is here expressed, with that description of the millennial glory, contained in the xxi st and xxii d chapters of this book,—wherein God is exhibited, as in this passage likewise, as dwelling with his church (xxi. 3) in the New Jerusalem; whose servants are represented (xxii. 3, 4) as serving him continually, neither enduring any more sorrow, nor crying, nor pain, because God shall wipe away all tears from their eyes (xxi. 4) ; and the Lamb, who is the light of the city, shall feed them and shall lead them to waters of life (xxi. 6, and xxii. 1), and they shall reign for ever and ever.

We are presented, in verse 14, with a confirmation of that fundamental doctrine of the Christian religion, that it is the blood of Christ alone that can cleanse from all sin, and that it is through much tribulation that we can be rendered participators of the blessings of that happy period. (see also chap. 1. 5.)

CHAPTERS VIII. AND IX.

Commencement of Trumpet History, or Eastern Branch of the Roman Empire.

THE history of the seals, and the first of the three main prophecies having been terminated, this chapter introduces that of the trumpets, or second series, in the Apostle's vision.

1 *And when he had opened the seventh seal, there was silence in heaven about the space of half an hour.*

The silence in heaven which immediately follows the opening of the seventh seal, which it is to be supposed, as usual, would have contained

2 *And I saw the seven angels which stood before God ; and to them were given seven trumpets.*

the peculiar subject of that seal, intimates to us that the particulars are reserved for another portion of the prophecy ; and that now the Apostle is about to begin a new act in the Apocalyptic drama, which should be introduced as events consequent upon the sounding of the seven trumpets, given to the seven angels, and which must receive their interpretation in the eastern branch of the Roman Empire.

There is a prefatory introduction to this, as to every chronological prophecy contained in this book, which seems to have been adopted as a Divine expedient, to act as a landmark to the comprehension of its structure.

If these verses be read in a parenthesis, it will be found that their omission altogether does not interfere with the sense of the passage ; but that the commencement of the sixth verse is closely connected with the latter clause of the second. In

3 *And another angel came and stood at the altar, having a golden censer ; and there was given unto him much incense, that he should offer it with the prayers of all saints upon the golden altar which was before the throne.*

4 *And the smoke of the incense, which came with the prayers of the saints, ascended up before God out of the angel's hand.*

this parenthesis, then, is contained an introduction to the whole; but especially taking a prophetic glance at the seventh trumpet, when the earthquake takes place, mentioned in chap. xi. 19, and also is detailed with other accompaniments of Divine vengeance, at the pouring out of the seventh vial, in chap. xvi. The angel standing at the altar, having the golden censer, with much incense, represents our Lord in his character of High Priest. The symbols employed, carry us back to Leviticus xvi. 12, 13; and a comparison of the two passages leads us to conclude, that the event referred to, and typified by this emblem is the day of atonement. The seventh trumpet answers the same end, in the dispensations of God to the Gentile church, as the day of atonement did to Israel. It is the day of vengeance and year of recompence, as it is written in Isaiah lxiii. 4 : " The day of vengeance is in mine heart, and the year of my redeemed is come." See also Isaiah xxxiv. 8.

5. And the angel took the censer, and filled it with fire of the altar and cast it into the earth : and there were voices, and thunderings, and lightnings, and an earthquake.

The trumpets exclusively apply to the eastern branch of the Roman empire, being one of the three parts into which Constantine the Great divided it; and hence the frequent recurrence of the expression, peculiar to the trumpet history, of the third part of the earth, the third part of men, &c. Agreeably, therefore, to this rule, we interpret the first trumpet to signify the Gothic eruption in the reign of the emperor Valens, A.D. 376.

6 And the seven angels which had the seven trumpets prepared themselves to sound.

7 The first angel sounded and there followed hail and fire mingled with blood, and they were cast upon the earth : and the third part of trees was burnt up, and all green grass was burnt up.

Its sounding was followed by hail and fire mingled with blood. Hail, in symbolic language, denotes war from a northern quarter, (hail being supposed to generate in the north) ; and fire and blood accompanying it, point out the destructive character of the warfare which should ensue. The descent of this hail upon the trees, and grass, is strictly consistent with the analogy of the symbol, and denotes the ruin brought upon the inhabitants of the empire. In the year 376, the Visigoths driven from their possessions to the north of the Danube, by an invasion of the Huns, received permission of Valens to settle themselves in the Roman dominions; which they had scarcely effected, before they rose up in arms against the Roman power, and, after defeating the general sent against them, ravaged the whole country south of the Danube. Uniting their forces with the Ostrogoths and other barbarians, whom they invited to cross the Danube, in two years after their entrance, they defeated and slew the emperor Valens at the battle of Adrianople; and, after destroying two-thirds of his army, desolated the provinces as far as the confines of Italy. They were afterwards driven back by the emperor Theodosius; but his death, occurring January 395, prepared the way for another Gothic invasion, contained in the second trumpet *.

8 *And the second angel sounded, and as it were a great mountain burning with fire was cast into the sea: and the third part of the sea became blood:*

9 *And the third part of the creatures which were in the sea, and had life, died; and the third part of the ships were destroyed.*

A mountain is often used in Scripture, to describe a destroying power; as in Zech. iv. 7, and in Jer. li. 25. It may either receive a personal application, as in the first instance, where the infidel king is addressed; or the more usual signification attached to the figure in symbolic language, may be applied in the interpretation of this second trumpet: in this sense, it would mean a kingdom. In the year following the death of Theodosius the Great, Alaric, the Goth came in upon the Greek provinces like a volcano. In describing which irruption, Gibbon says (chap. xxx), "The fields of Phocis and Bœotia were covered by a deluge of barbarians: the whole territory of Attica, from the promontory of Sunium, to the town of Megara, was blasted with their baneful presence, and Athens itself resembled the bleeding and empty skin of a slaughtered victim. Corinth, Argos, Sparta, yielded without resistance to the arms of the Goths; and the most fortunate of the inhabitants were saved by death, from beholding the slavery of their families, and the conflagration of their cities." It is well known, that whole nations transported themselves in these irruptions, with their families and property, into the invaded

* See Gibbon, chap. xxvi.

territories, carrying fire and sword and desolation wherever they came : which terrible and overwhelming destruction could scarcely receive a more comprehensive symbol, than a great mountain burning with fire being cast into the sea.

The sea being turned into blood, in ver. 8, clearly directs our attention, in solving this emblem, to the extinction of human life, in the third part of the Roman earth ; and the destruction of the third part of ships, in ver. 9, to the utter annihilation of all civil and ecclesiastical establishments, which sunk beneath the overpowering violence of these barbarous invaders.

A star, agreeably to the interpretation of our Lord himself (chap. i. 20), means a minister of religion ; and consistently with the dictionary of the symbolic language, as laid down in the preface, we are led to expect the apostacy of a conspicuous head in the ecclesiastical hemisphere, whose defection from the true doctrine should operate with peculiar malignancy on the church, emblematized by the rivers and fountains of waters, as the source and streams of Christian knowledge, which are re-

10 *And the third angel sounded, and there fell a great star from heaven, burning as it were a lamp, and it fell upon the third part of the rivers, and upon the fountains of waters.*

11 *And the name of the star is called Wormwood ; and the third part of the waters became wormwood ; and many men died of the waters, because they were made bitter.*

presented in the text as becoming so polluted as to cause men to die. The star is denominated Wormwood, to accord with the accuracy of the figure, and to express more fully the deleterious and pernicious character of his false doctrine. In directing our researches, therefore, into the history of the Eastern Church for such a defaulter, we find Nestorius, Bishop of Constantinople, present himself to our view, as a singular fulfilment of this prediction. Eusebius informs us[*], that he was termed "the Father of Blasphemy ; and that were he to compose a history of the heresies of the church, he should begin with the impious Nestorius, whose false doctrine occasioned a great dissension in the Constantinopolitan church ;" and he adds, " the war of the churches had its origin from hence ; and this adulterate coin, stamped

---

[*] See Eusebius Ecclesiast. Hist. of Evagrius Scholasticus, Lib. i. ch. 2—7.